Research in the
Early Years

Research in the Early Years:

A step-by-step guide

Pam Jarvis, Stephen Newman,
Wendy Holland and
Jane George

PEARSON

Harlow, England • London • New York • Boston • San Francisco • Toronto • Sydney
Auckland • Singapore • Hong Kong • Tokyo • Seoul • Taipei • New Delhi
Cape Town • São Paulo • Mexico City • Madrid • Amsterdam • Munich • Paris • Milan

Pearson Education Limited
Edinburgh Gate
Harlow
Essex CM20 2JE
England

and Associated Companies throughout the world

Visit us on the World Wide Web at:
www.pearson.com/uk

First published 2012

© Pearson Education Limited 2012

ISBN 978-1-4082-5407-3

British Library Cataloguing-in-Publication Data
A catalogue record for this book is available from the British Library

Library of Congress Cataloging-in-Publication Data
Research in the early years: a step-by-step guide / Pam Jarvis . . . [et al.].
    p. cm.
  Includes index.
  ISBN 978-1-4082-5407-3 (pbk.)
 1. Early childhood education—Research—Methodology. 2. Child
development—Research—Methodology.   I. Jarvis, Pam.
  LB1139.23.R44 2012
  372.21072—dc23

                                        2012006945

10 9 8 7 6 5 4 3 2 1
16 15 14 13 12

Typeset in 10.25/14 pt Interstate Light by 73
Printed and bound in Great Britain by Henry Ling, at the Dorset Press, Dorchester, Dorset.

From Pam Jarvis
For Lennon, who arrived first: amazing, just the way you are

From Stephen Newman
For all those who have supported and encouraged me on my
'research journeys'

From Wendy Holland
For Adam, creative and curious from the very beginning

From Jane George
To Sarah and Graham who are my first, best research project

Contents

Preface

This book started its life as a very small glint in my eye when I was a PhD student in a busy education studies department between 2001 and 2004, supplementing my bursary by supervising dissertations for a wide range of students on Early Childhood Studies and Education programmes. As time went by, I began to realise that, in general, my research students experienced a range of common issues at specific points of their process through dissertation/practitioner research modules; that students in the same 'category' (for example, fulltime or parttime, classroom or other Early Years setting, different subjects of previous study) tended to have similar experiences, and that there was a range of relatively predictable differences between students in different categories. Above all, I became increasingly aware that many of my research module tutees had not entered a degree in childhood studies or education in the realisation that they would be called upon to undertake independent research in the later stages of their degree. As a result, many entered dissertation or practitioner research modules feeling quite daunted by the processes they were directed to undertake, and my first, most important role was to support them through these concerns.

Having moved through my own undergraduate experience via a BSc (Hons) in Psychology, a track which students enter in the full realisation that they are going to be required to undertake increasingly independent research activities, it took me a while to fully orient to my students' concerns, not least because most of the sources for undergraduates on the topic of 'doing research' did not seem designed to speak to the typical student with whom I was working. It was as this realisation dawned that I began to think: '*someone* ought to write a book that speaks directly to these students', but at that point, immersed in my own doctoral research and the subsequent challenge of constructing a thesis, it did not occur to me that the 'someone' would ever be me.

However, once I had finally finished my thesis and received my PhD, I was subsequently appointed to a role where my principal day-to-day round consisted of supervising undergraduate and Master's student research, alongside several colleagues. As I got to know my colleagues better, in particular through discussion of our teaching experiences, I began to realise that much of our conversation reiterated issues that I had identified several years previously: that

Early Years and Education students were frequently daunted by the prospect of 'doing research', and that the majority of books on the market that attempted to deal with this topic did not effectively recognise this fundamental issue. An additional impetus to write '*the* research book' for students in Early Years roles studying on dissertation and practitioner research modules came from my growing recognition that I was working with a team of individuals whose dedication and diversity of previous experience gave them an integral collective strength: classroom teachers, Early Years practitioners, experienced researchers, a social scientist and a librarian, who, viewed as a group, had constructed myriad dissertations and theses on a wide range of under- and post-graduate degrees, had many 'person-years' of experience supporting student research, and a wide range of previous publications. So, at the end of 2008, I said to Stephen Newman, Jane George and Wendy Holland: 'Why don't we . . . .' and all accepted enthusiastically.

Our first conversations relating to 'the book' all reiterated common experiences that we had had with a wide range of students over our many collective years of dissertation supervision, and eventually I said, 'So why not tell the story of the Early Years student dissertation through a set of example students, who will lead our readers through all the experiences we are discussing here?' This was enthusiastically taken up, particularly by Wendy, who is largely responsible for the excellent characterisation that you will find throughout the book, but particularly in Chapter 6. In fact, during a conversation about 'Sunil' at the point we were putting this chapter together, she was talking about his progress with such enthusiasm that I finally said, 'Wendy . . . you do remember we made him up, don't you?' at which we both laughed until we cried. I truly believe that creating these characters and moving them through their dissertation/practitioner research modules made this one of the most enjoyable experiences of creating a book on the trials, tribulations and triumphs of the 'undergraduate research in Early Years' process that authors in this arena could ever experience, and we hope that some of the pleasure that we took in this is communicated to you, the reader.

I should at this point thank my son, Andrew Jarvis, currently studying for his own PhD in Mechanical Engineering who, in his other persona as an artist (and whose artistic products at different stages of his development can be found in nearly every room of my house) agreed to give some amount of 'flesh' to our students in the production of the pictures that you will find in this book. Once we had finished the pen portraits that you will find in Chapter 1, and had received Andrew's drawings of the people associated with these, we found that by and large these imaginary students took over the construction of the chapters, leading us through the text similarly to the ways in which generations of *real* students have led us through their dissertations. This reversal of the traditional tutor–student role perennially creates the immortal magic of the dissertation module. However, the majority of undergraduate students tend only to fully grasp this phenomenon when they get to the end and hold their own independent creation, the bound dissertation, in their hand for the very first time, gazing at their name on the title page!

We hope that with 'Ellie', 'Nick', 'Sunil' and 'Florentyna' to accompany you on your journey through your dissertation (alongside your all-important dissertation tutor) you will never feel completely alone, as they can sit beside you as you type long into the night on your laptop, or laboriously sort papers into piles on your living room floor, or browse through resources in your college library. Many of their experiences are likely to mirror yours, and, as such, it would be a good idea to begin with a plan to steadily read through this book as you move through your dissertation, focusing on the chapter that is relevant to each stage, just as you begin to move into it.

Chapter 1, Planning and preparation: your Early Years research project introduces 'Ellie', 'Nick', 'Sunil' and 'Florentyna' and focuses on how they put their initial ideas together to identify a dissertation topic. The chapter explores issues relating to the professional reflection and ethical practice that are required to underpin student research processes from the very beginning.

Chapter 2, Reading for research: efficient use of your access to an academic library finds our example students moving into the library to begin the reading they need to do to underpin their literature review, using both paper-based and electronic resources. You will find that they have very different levels of experience of searching for academic resources, depending on their previous experiences of both study and life in general.

Chapter 3, The literature review and sectioning the project write-up focuses upon putting the literature review together, in particular writing 'thematically' and avoiding common pitfalls that can unnecessarily reduce a final dissertation grade. The sections of the typical undergraduate student research report are introduced in this chapter to help readers organise their written drafts from the very beginning of the write-up process.

Chapter 4, Introduction to methodology moves gently into research terminology, introducing concepts of qualitative and quantitative research, triangulation, sampling and action research. It focuses upon surveys and interviews, with a brief introduction to the multi-method concept of 'Mosaic', which is designed to facilitate young children's authentic participation in the research process.

Chapter 5, Observation-based research in the Early Years takes a focused approach to observation. This is by far the most popular method used within Early Years research, and if properly done has the potential to be the most illuminating when research is undertaken with very young children. A wide range of types and methods of observation are considered including the Leuven Child Involvement Scale, and the practitioner observation schedules of ECERS (Early Childhood Environment Rating Scales) and ITERS-R (Infant-Toddler Environment Rating Scale), and how these may be flexibly used in student research. Finally, there is an in-depth discussion of thematic analysis of qualitative observation data.

Chapter 6, Putting research methods into action follows 'Ellie', 'Nick', 'Sunil' and 'Florentyna' as they move through their research processes in a variety of settings using a variety of research methods with varying levels of success. It considers how they solve some of the problems that arise, and work around others. The focus is upon carrying out student research in a range of busy Early Years settings in which the researcher has to simultaneously carry out their everyday work and fit research activities into the setting rather than vice versa. All of our example students find in very different ways that research activities have the potential to produce a surprisingly wide range of responses from both children and colleagues, some problematic and some positive.

Chapter 7, Presenting your data finds our example students thinking about how they are going to present their data within their dissertation or practitioner research report. This chapter will take you through a range of ways to present data, in particular how to 'showcase' your data in ways that aid the reader's understanding, rather than overwhelming them with irrelevant detail.

Chapter 8, Discussing and concluding: placing your findings within the frame of Early Years research moves towards the final stages of the write-up – the discussion and conclusion. The chapter recognises that this is likely to be the stage of the process that students find most challenging, and you will again meet our example students problem-solving as they attempt to write critically and analytically through revisiting the literature, to consider issues relating to reliability/validity/representativeness as these impact on their research, and reflect upon ways that their research processes have developed their own practice, and the practice within their settings.

Chapter 9, Presentation of report: gaining marks for 'readability' attempts to provide a range of answers to that question dissertation tutors are so often asked in the final tutorial: 'How do I make *my* dissertation stand out from the crowd?' Careful organisation of text and referencing are considered, alongside writing a succinct, informative abstract; creating cohesion throughout the text of a dissertation/practitioner research report; use of appendices and making considered stylistic choices. Common pitfalls that are easy to avoid, but which may depress a potential grade, are highlighted throughout this chapter.

We wish you all the best with your dissertation/practitioner research assignment, and hope that you will, at the end of your studies, look back fondly upon a range of challenging but stimulating processes that developed both your professional and personal skills of reflection and analysis. We also hope that taking your first walk on the long road to becoming a lifelong reflective practitioner alongside 'Nick', 'Ellie', 'Florentyna' and 'Sunil' will be both instructive and enjoyable.

We launch this book with the wish that you will as a reader find as much enjoyment in its pages as we had as writers in putting the text together. Good luck with your research!

Pam Jarvis

2012

Foreword

Recent years have seen a great deal of attention paid in the United Kingdom by first the New Labour and currently the coalition government to research regarding young children and their early life experiences. This research has highlighted the significance of the earliest years to long-term achievement and well-being and the importance of a well trained, reflective, early childhood work-force (see, for example, Sylva *et al.*, 2010). This research has also emphasised the difference that graduates make to outcomes for young children. This has resulted in considerable growth in undergraduate and postgraduate courses for those interested in becoming early childhood practitioners and for those who already work in the field but who lack a graduate level qualification. Most such courses include a research project/dissertation as a key way of enabling students to develop the research, reflection and analytical skills which are at the core of understanding children and improving practice.

Whilst students understand the importance of research as part of their academic and professional development, many also approach the research project/dissertation with some degree of trepidation. A growing number of books deal with the complexities of research with young children and provide guidance on how to plan, carry out and write up an early childhood research project. This is the only one I know, however, that engages with students' anxieties and supports them on their journey as they undertake their research project/dissertation.

The approach taken by the authors is a very distinctive one and centres around fictional case studies of some students whose backgrounds and experiences many will recognise as characteristic of those who carry out Early Years research projects as part of their undergraduate studies. We follow these fictional students and the issues they encounter throughout the research journey.

Early in the book, students are supported with efficient research planning and with what to do and who to turn to when faced by those all too familiar but awful moments of feeling at sea in the literature. Overcoming those problems, help is provided with creating a literature review that is reflective and analytical and which avoids the dangers of the shopping list of authors and references which is common in many undergraduate dissertations.

Methodological matters are covered at some length and in some detail, with clarification of the often confused difference between methodology, methods and procedures. Given that the focus is very much on exploring research from the perspective of part-time students who are seeking to improve their own practice and that in their settings, the value of action research in impacting on practice is usefully highlighted.

Detailed discussion of questionnaires, interviews and observations follows. Students often favour questionnaires and these are discussed in some depth together with the issues associated with their use in qualitative research. Different types of interviews are also outlined in ways which support the student researcher. A range of approaches to observation are discussed and helpful guidance is provided on approaches to analysis. Awareness of ethical issues in research involving children has increased in recent years and this is rightly reflected in discussions surrounding young children's consent.

There is recognition of the way in which students (and more experienced researchers) commonly feel overwhelmed as they engage in their research and seek to juggle methodological concerns, time constraints and professional and practice considerations. All of this should be reassuring to readers in that such feelings are often overlooked in other texts about the research process. The case studies give a real sense of the types of issues that are faced by students during the 'doing' of research and should help with the feelings of isolation.

Students will find a great deal more detail than is found in most similar books about how to present data and the things to consider when doing so. A wide range of charts and graphs are explained together with the possible pitfalls associated with them, especially when used in association with the kinds of qualitative research that students typically carry out as part of their early childhood projects/dissertations. There is encouragement and support with reflecting on and analysing the methods of data collection used. As highlighted by the authors, often the best dissertations are the ones that show real insight in reflecting on the research journey. I frequently comment to my own students that their best writing often concerns their research 'going wrong'!

Finally, students are helped with the overall presentation of the dissertation. The importance of clarity, accuracy, care, organisation and signposting are emphasised and indeed cannot be overstated. Attention is drawn to the importance of reviewing the title of the dissertation to ensure that what was often decided some time earlier is still appropriate as the title of the dissertation to be submitted – something which spoke readily to me as someone who failed to do just this with the title of my doctoral thesis! The tips on what to do and what not to do, which words to use and which to avoid, will also be helpful for students and highlight the experience and expertise of the authors.

Carrying out research in early childhood is rewarding but it can also feel daunting for many students. This book should help them to know that they are not alone in the challenges they face and should provide them with insights which give them confidence and enable them to succeed.

Reference

Sylva, K., Melhuish, E., Sammons, P., Siraj-Blatchford, I. and Taggart, B. (2010) *Early Childhood Matters*, London: Routledge.

Dr Ian Barron
Centre for Cultural Studies of Children and Childhood,
Educational and Social Research Institute,
Manchester Metropolitan University.

Biographical details

Ian has had a variety of experiences in the early childhood field, including work in primary schools in inner London and Leeds and two headship posts, one of a nursery school and the other of an infant school. He has also worked in colleges of further and higher education.

Since joining Manchester Metropolitan University (MMU) in 2000, Ian has had a variety of roles in the Institute of Education. He was part of the MMU Project Team that developed *Birth to Three Matters* for the DfES/Sure Start. He has been a member of a number of DfE advisory groups concerned with developments in the early childhood area. Ian's research interests are in early childhood generally and in aspects of identity (especially gender and ethnicity). He is a member of the Centre for Cultural Studies of Children and Childhood within the Educational and Social Research Institute at MMU.

Ian is also Vice-Chair of the national Early Childhood Studies Degrees Network and was co-chair of the group which developed a QAA Subject Benchmark for Early Childhood Studies.

About the authors

Dr Pam Jarvis is a graduate psychologist, social scientist and educational researcher, with many years of experience of creating and teaching developmental, social science and social policy modules for Education/Child Development programmes for community, further and higher education, most recently within the area of Early Years Professional training. She has Qualified Teacher Status and has taught in school within her specialist subject areas of psychology, sociology and history. She is currently working as a Senior Lecturer in the McMillan School of Teaching, Health and Care, Bradford College, and as an Open University tutor, supporting education and child development students on a wide range of programmes at undergraduate and Master's level. She is also an active researcher, and has recently finished a piece of historical research on the life and work of Early Years practice pioneer Margaret McMillan. She was awarded a PhD by Leeds Metropolitan University in 2005 for her thesis 'The Role of Rough and Tumble Play in Children's Social and Gender Role Development in The Early Years of Primary School'. Her recent publications include:

Jarvis, P. (2010) 'Born to Play': The biocultural roots of 'rough and tumble' play, and its impact upon human development. In P. Broadhead, J. Howard and E. Wood (eds), *Play and learning in early years settings; from research to practice*, 61–78, London: Sage.

Brock, A., Dodds, S., Jarvis, P. and Olusoga, Y. (2009) *Perspectives on Play: Learning for Life*, Harlow: Pearson Education.

Jarvis, P. (2009) Play, narrative and learning in education: a biocultural perspective, *Educational and Child Psychology*, 26 (2): 66–76.

Dr Stephen Newman has many years of experience of teaching in secondary and higher education. He has Qualified Teacher Status. He was formerly the Course Leader for MA and MEd programmes in the McMillan School of Teaching, Health and Care at Bradford College University Centre, and is currently a Senior Lecturer in Education and Continuing Professional Development at Leeds Metropolitan University, working with students on undergraduate, Master's and Doctoral courses. His particular interest is philosophy and, in particular, the philosophy of Ludwig Wittgenstein. He was awarded a PhD by The University of

Sheffield in 1997 for his thesis on teacher education and professional development, which was subsequently published. His recent publications include:

Newman, S. and Jahdi, K. (2009) Marketisation of education: marketing, rheto-
ric and reality, *Journal of Further and Higher Education*, 33 (1): 1–11.

Wendy Holland (MA) has experience of teaching in mainstream nurseries, primary and special schools for over thirty years. From the 1970s onwards, her
focus has been around inclusive provision and practice for childen 0 to 8 years.
Through the establishment of mother and toddler groups and playgroups for
children with particular needs, integrated mainstream provision for hearing
and hearing impaired nursery and primary-aged children, she has pursued her
particular interests around the inclusion of parents/carers in the caring and
educative process. The importance of the role of reflective practitioner as an
agent for change is another of her interests and she is currently involved in the
training and assessing of Early Years Professionals at Bradford College. She
is also working at present in the Teaching, Health and Care sector at Bradford
College developing and producing modules for the BA (Hons) with Qualified
Teacher Status degree and the BEd Studies degree, alongside supporting students engaged in a range of undergraduate and Master's level programmes. Her
recent publications include:

Holland, W. (2009) The Patchwork Quilt. In G. Murphy and M. Power (eds),
A story to tell, 25–32, Stoke-on-Trent: Trentham Books.

Jarvis, P., George, J. and Holland, W. (2010) *The Early Years Professional's
Complete Companion*, Harlow: Pearson Longman.

Jarvis, P. and Holland, W. (2011) The Early Years Professional and the Children's
Centre: at the hub of the 'Big Society'? In A. Brock and C. Rankin (eds), *Making
it work for the child: professionalism for the early years interdisciplinary team*,
79–92, London: Continuum.

Jane George (MEd) has extensive experience in the voluntary sector, in toddler
groups and playgroups and managing and teaching for the Pre-School Learning
Alliance. She has worked in Community Education developing and delivering
Parent and Toddler at Play classes in areas of social deprivation and to various
cultural groups. Working in colleges across West Yorkshire, she has developed
and delivered a variety of Early Years programmes across the range of further
and higher education. She was awarded an MEd in 2002. In her current role of
Programme Manager for Early Years, Health and Care at Bradford College she
manages the curriculum across the full range of Further and Higher Education
programmes in Early Years and Health and Care, including the Foundation

Degree in Early Years; the BA Hons Early Childhood Studies/Early Years Practice; the Master's in Early Years Practice and all four Early Years Professional Status Pathways. Her recent publications include:

Jarvis, P. and George, J. (2008) Play, Learning for Life: the vital role of play in human development. In A. Brock, S. Dodds, P. Jarvis and Y. Olusoga (eds), *Perspectives on Play: Learning for Life,* 251-71, Harlow: Pearson Longman.

Jarvis, P. and George, J. (2010) Thinking it Through: Rough and Tumble Play. In J. Moyles (ed.), *Thinking it through: Reflecting on playful pedagogy in the early years,* 164-78, Buckingham: OU Press.

Dr Clive Opie is the Dean of the McMillan School of Teaching, Health and Care at Bradford College. He has been involved in the Early Years Professional Status initiative since its inception, taking on the role of Chair of the EYPS Executive Committee while Deputy Director of the Institute of Education at Manchester Metropolitan University. His research interests have centred on the use of IT to support and enhance teaching and learning in a range of settings, e.g. schools, and undergraduate and postgraduate degree courses. He has had substantial experience of teaching at Master's level in the area of research procedures and data analysis. His current work revolves around developing an Enhanced Partnership with schools and his most recent paper 'Developing ITE without wholesale change to practice – an Enhanced Partnership' was presented at the conference on Re-Imagining Initial Teacher Education, Dublin (2011). Other relevant publications include a text jointly authored with Judith Bell, *Learning from Research – Getting More from your Data*, Open University (2002) and acting as editor/author for *Doing Educational Research – A Guide for First Time Researchers*, Sage (2004).

Rónán O'Beirne is director for learning development at Bradford College, responsible for four college libraries, the digital media service and the college's virtual research and learning environments. He also has a remit to lead and develop the college research community of approximately 50 staff active in research.

Throughout his career in librarianship Rónán has worked in public, academic and specialist libraries. He has also worked as a consultant for various agencies including the University for Industry, BECTA and the European Commission, developing a track record of leading-edge research in educational metadata. A pioneer in community networking, he has worked with a range of communities and neighbourhoods to exploit technology to empower citizens. For seven years he was internet editor on the international journal *Reference Reviews*, and for two years was editor-in-chief of the *International Journal of Information*

Literacy. In 2009 he won the UK National Information Literacy Practitioner Award for his work on information literacy and digital citizenship.

Rónán is a governor of the Appleton Academy, an all-through academy specialising in science and sport; he is also a Director of the UKRC – Resource Centre for Women in Science Engineering and Technology. His current research interests include learner-generated contexts, educational informatics and research ethics. He holds a BA degree in librarianship, an MEd qualification in computer-supported collaborative learning and is currently undertaking the EdD doctorate programme at University of Sheffield. Rónán is chair of the national Library and Information Research Group and a Fellow of the Chartered Institute of Library and Information Professionals. His recent publications include:

O'Beirne, R. (2010) *From lending to learning: the development and extension of public libraries*, Oxford: Chandos.

Acknowledgements

Authors Acknowledgements

For all of our research students over the years whose experiences have been recounted through 'Ellie', 'Nick', 'Sunil' and 'Florentyna': while too numerous to name individually, we hope that you will all recognise yourself in these pages, and maybe even be inspired to re-read that successful dissertation with pride. Heartfelt thanks to one and all for being the inspiration for this book, and the source of much of our own continuing professional development.

Pam Jarvis would also like to briefly acknowledge the implicit contribution of Lennon, her first grandchild, who arrived during the months when the final drafts of the chapters were being written and edited, providing her with a wealth of contemporary, ongoing practical observations of the miracle of the first year of human development in action.

Special thanks also go to Andrew Jarvis who created the cartoons that feature throughout the book

Pam Jarvis, Stephen Newman, Wendy Holland and Jane George

2012

Publisher's Acknowledgements

We are grateful to the following for permission to reproduce copyright material:

Figures
Figure 3.1 from *Constructing a good dissertation: A practical guide to finishing a masters, MBA or PhD on schedule*, Exactica (Hoftsee, E. 2006) p. 96; Cartoons © Andrew Jarvis, 2012.

Tables
Table on page 133 from *Qualitative Data Analysis: A Sourcebook of New Methods*, Publications Inc (Miles, MB and Huberman, AM. 1984) p. 89, Reproduced with permission of SAGE PUBLICATIONS INC BOOKS in the format Tradebook and Other book via Copyright Clearance Center; Table on page 139 from Scatter Graph, http://www.mathsrevision.net/gcse/pages.php?page=10, Reproduced by permission of RevisionWorld http://www.revisionworld.co.uk/

Text
Case Study on page 64 from Understanding Co-Teaching Components (Figure 1), *Teaching Exceptional Children*, Vol. 33(4), pp. 40–47. (Gately, S. and Gately, F. 2001), Copyright 2001 the Council for Exceptional Children. Reprinted with permission; Exhibits on pages 94–95, pages 95–97 after *Infant/ Toddler Environment Rating Scale, Revised Edition Manual*, Teachers College Press. (Harms, T., Cryer, D. and Clifford, R. M. 2006), Reprinted by permission of the Publisher. Copyright © 2005 by Thelma Harms, Richard M. Clifford, and Deborah Reid Cryer. All rights reserved.

In some instances we have been unable to trace the owners of copyright material, and we would appreciate any information that would enable us to do so.

Chapter 1
Planning and preparation: your Early Years research project

Pam Jarvis, Wendy Holland and Jane George

Introduction

This chapter will introduce the concept of research in Early Years settings and the way that this book intends to support those who work within schools, nurseries and other Early Years care and education settings through their undergraduate research modules. It will cover:

- Choosing and refining a topic
- The concept of 'reflective practice'
- Basic introductions to:
  - Reliability
  - Validity
  - Representativeness
  - Objectivity
  - Research ethics
  - Current debates arising from the increasing number of practitioner research projects in Early Years settings

If you are reading this book it is likely that you are either looking forward to starting, or have just started a dissertation or practitioner research project. Writing between five and ten thousand words on a topic that you are expected to select for yourself can be a daunting prospect, and we hope that we can help you to hone your abilities to manage yourself through this experience, and emerge with a positive result.

First of all, remember that this is a project that you have to undertake in small steps. When students first look at the prospect of researching and writing a dissertation, it often seems that there are so many things to think about it will never get done, but if you take it in small 'chunks' you will find it less over-whelming. As the old saying proposes: 'How do you eat an elephant? One bite at a time.'

You will need to set goals, organise, schedule and prioritise so you can complete your project within the time available; this book will help you in this respect.

Introducing . . .

We have constructed four example students, who are composites of people we have all known over our collective years of working with students completing dissertations and practitioner research projects. They will begin their research module in this chapter and then we will follow them through the book as they move through their projects meeting a range of problems and solutions, and pitfalls and triumphs.

Ellie

. . . is a final year BA (Hons) Early Childhood Studies student embarking upon a 30 credit, level 6 dissertation module. She is 37 years old and has worked in childcare since achieving her NNEB when she was 18. She has approached her degree via part-time study along the Foundation Degree route, obtaining day release from her work. She is currently deputy manager in a private day-care setting, and is married with two daughters aged 7 and 10. She has really taken the idea of reflection to heart, but suffers from 'analysis paralysis'! She is beginning to question everything in her employment environment, and has attempted to set into action a spiral of improvements; however, she finds it difficult to identify stages of action and 'rest' points. She will submit a 6000-word dissertation.

Nick

. . . is a Graduate Teacher Training Programme (GTP) student embarking upon a 40 credit, level 6 dissertation module. He was made redundant from his job in financial services three years ago. He is 45 years old, and lives with his partner. Their children are currently at university. He has been employed in a primary school (reception class) as a non-qualified teacher with a view to working towards taking on the role of maths co-ordinator when he completes his training. His colleagues and mentors think highly of him, but he lacks confidence in his own ability. He was a very high achiever in his previous career and found working through the process of redundancy very difficult. He sets very high standards for himself and others. Nick will submit a 10,000-word dissertation.

Florentyna

. . . is now in the final year of her Foundation Degree in Early Years, embarking on a 30 credit, level 5 practitioner research module. She is 30 years old, and was brought up in Eastern Europe; her nation is now part of the European Union. She speaks English as an additional language, and obtained a sociology and law degree in her native country. She came to the UK three years ago, learning to speak and write English through a programme of college courses. She has now settled down with her English partner and plans to stay in the UK. She started her Foundation Degree in Early Years when she was given paid employment by her local children's centre, after a short period as a volunteer language support worker. Florentyna wishes to move on into a full BA top-up once she has finished her FD, and is aiming for an overall distinction. Practitioner research is a double module, so her grade for this is pivotal within her overall performance. Florentyna will submit a 5000-word practitioner research assignment.

Sunil

. . . is 25 years old and currently enrolled on the Registered Teacher Training Programme (RTP) at his local university, in which he will be taking a 20 credit, level 6 practitioner research module. He is working in a nursery/reception classroom as a language support mentor. He is currently single, and has taken a circuitous employment route to his current studies that has involved a period spent in youth work (during which time he obtained a Foundation Degree in Child and Youth Studies), a part-time, temporary job supervising the breakfast club in the school where he currently works, followed by full-time employment as a language support learning mentor. Last year, Sunil completed a Higher Level Teaching Assistant Qualification. His employers now want him to obtain full Qualified Teacher Status, so he has enrolled on the 'top-up' year of the BA in Education Studies with QTS at his local university. Sunil thoroughly enjoys working with the children in the classroom, but he does not enjoy academic study at all. He disliked the volume of essay and report writing that he was required to complete for his Foundation Degree, and is looking forward to finishing with the least amount of additional stress. He is aiming for a bare pass on his 4000-word practitioner research assignment.

Choosing and refining a topic

There is, occasionally, a misconception among students, even among those who are Early Years subject specialists, that Early Years is an 'easy' arena for a dissertation focus. It is not uncommon for a dissertation tutorial to begin with a student presenting their research question as: *'What are the benefits of play in Early Years?'*, or: *'What significance does gender have in the Early Years?'* or: *'What is the importance of language in young children's thinking?'* These are just a few examples of conceptually huge research questions that students have expected to address within a three-month research period and a six thousand word dissertation!

When subsequently asked to define terms such as 'play', 'gender' or 'language' in relation to children's 'thinking', students begin to realise that although a young child has a limited history in terms of years and experience it does not automatically mean that the 'story of their journey so far' lacks a level of real complexity. Any attempt to unravel or interpret such young human behaviour in terms of its 'significance' or 'meaning' demands a depth of academic integrity which both challenges and rewards those who try.

Finding the right question(s) to ask is the starting point for any research journey. This in itself, however, can be fraught with difficulties, for it demands of the researcher the kind of honest reflection that some might find uncomfortable. What has triggered the student's interest in a particular focus? How does it reflect on them as an individual? Does it show significant bias for a particular viewpoint or the pressure of school/setting politics? Has the choice been made for more mundane, practical reasons such as time constraints and the need to meet course work deadlines? What might be the benefits and barriers to carrying out a piece of research on this topic in the relevant setting?

Sunil

. . . had misgivings about the recent changes in his workplace. It wasn't the school management as a whole that concerned him; the head teacher was fantastic, so full of energy and ideas; very committed to successive governments' drives on child poverty. When the inspectors had come to visit, he'd taken them on a tour of the local estate before they'd set foot inside the school! This year he was trialling a more 'creative' approach to the curriculum, which some staff opposed (although Sunil thought it was 'wicked'). However, Sunil was beginning to become rather anxious about the politics within the mixed nursery/reception class where he had been placed. This was one of the changes that the head wanted to introduce, and Sunil had been part of the new staff team. He knew he had a lot to learn, having never worked with such young children before. He was now finding out that rumour in the staff room had it that the reception class teacher and the nursery teacher didn't get on. Great! School politics; that's all he needed. His concern centred on the very different approaches both teachers had to their teaching. The nursery teacher, he knew from personal experience when her class joined with the reception children each day, had some belief in the central importance of play, as he himself espoused, based upon what he had observed in 'troubled' older children and what he had learned during his Foundation Degree. However, the reception teacher (who really saw herself as a Key Stage 2 teacher) believed in a much more formal approach.

The ongoing government changes didn't help either, as just prior to the summer holidays the school as a whole had been thrown into ferment by the announcement of changes upon changes to the current national guidelines. What would Sunil's research plans have to encompass? He did not seem to be getting any really straight answers. His college cohort had spent a couple of intense sessions being taken through the module handbook, sketching an outline of what they were expected to do, but Sunil found that type of teaching quite impenetrable. He had not found the time to ask for extra input and now the deadline for handing in his practitioner research proposal was fast approaching. He vaguely knew his dissertation tutor, but wasn't sure how 'relaxed' she'd be about hand-in dates! He desperately needed to come up with a question. He spent several of his short car journeys to and from work pondering this point and came up with a question he felt was a winner: 'The importance of play for boys in a mixed age nursery/reception class.' Sorted.

Reflection point

Do you think Sunil is 'sorted'? If not, make a list of some other aspects he needs to think about. It might be helpful to discuss this with other people in your research group and make a list together.

Florentyna

. . . did not want to come up with any old idea for her practitioner research proposal; she wanted the final product to be the type of original, 'stand out from the crowd' assignment that gets a top class mark. One of the reasons Florentyna had initially been inspired to volunteer at the local Children's Centre was her interest in the 'Sure Start' initiative in her new country, which she very much admired. Her English teacher's child used to attend the centre, and he had asked whether Florentyna might like to volunteer some of her time to help families from Eastern European nations using the centre, given that Florentyna spoke two Eastern European languages fluently and had a basic knowledge of German. The initial purpose for her voluntary work there had been both to help the families and to improve her own English but, now she was both speaking and writing quite fluently, her focus had moved on. She found that she really enjoyed working with all the children, joining in with their play and answering their questions; it really didn't seem like work but fun. By the time she accepted her paid role at the centre she knew that she no longer wanted to follow her initial ambition of becoming a lawyer; she wanted to work in Early Years. Florentyna and her partner had talked about opening their own childcare setting once she was fully trained.

The work to construct an outdoor play area had begun shortly after Florentyna first arrived at the centre. She had been fascinated at every stage, and began to read up on the topic of outdoor play in the college library. She began to question whether the safe surfaces, carefully purpose-designed play areas and bright plastic toys/apparatus really created the best environment for the children. She has recently been reading up on European ideas on Forest Schools (the ability to read in three 'and a half' languages really helped here); and her thinking moved towards suggesting some changes which she could study and evaluate for her practitioner research project.

However, she finds some members of staff's attitudes to outdoor play somewhat negative, while others tend to be over-directive. She is also aware of her current quite junior role in the setting, and concerned about how she will acquire agreement to putting her ideas into action. She does not want any emerging problems to impact on her ability to 'get the job done', as this may in turn impact upon her potential grade.

Reflection point

If you were Florentyna, what points do you think you might include in a comparison of benefits and barriers in carrying out *this* piece of research in *this* setting?

Ellie

. . . emerges from her first tutorial with her tutor with her mind whirling. As deputy manager she has been put in charge of organising the key person system at her setting, and has found this quite challenging. She initially felt that using her work on this aspect might be a good focus for her disserta-tion, but now she is not so sure. When she took over the role she felt that the system was chaotic, so she was determined to completely revamp the whole thing. She started by instigating a system where the children chose their own key person, but this fell apart when it caused problems between the staff as some were getting more than their fair share of 'key children' and started to complain about inequality of workload. Her tutor has suggested that Ellie might be able to make some very gradual changes and study these through 'Action Research', but this process seemed to be far too slow for Ellie. She suspects that it will also be perceived as too slow by her manager and area manager, who are expecting quick results. She begins to wonder whether she should pick another topic.

Reflection point

What do you think? Should Ellie pick another topic or should she try to refine her original ideas? What would you advise her to do if she was a fellow student in your research group?

Nick

. . . has already tried to make a start on his dissertation topic over the summer holidays. He feels that the mathematics skills of some of the other staff in his school, particularly the support staff, are very poor, and he wanted to carry out some numeracy training with them, and then measure the impact that this has upon their work with the children. He has not designed the 'work with the children' aspect of the study as yet, but he did send out a questionnaire (to be returned in the last week of the summer term) for staff to attempt some mathematics questions so he can assess their current skills. The first problem that he brings to his tutor is that he didn't get any back and, when he asked why, people made a variety of excuses.

▶

Nick's tutor asks him to consider why he thinks that might have happened, and how Nick might refine his idea so he can get the project properly 'up and running'.

Reflection point

If you were Nick, what conclusions would you come to?

What is reflective practice? An introduction

Later on in this book you will meet methodologies based on reflective practice, in particular the process of 'Action Research' which is a regime of practice development through reflection. At this point, we are going to introduce you to a basic set of useful steps for reflection, which will help you focus on aspects of your practice that you feel that you can improve, and then to go through a process of questioning yourself:

- *Description:* What happened? Simply describing the events can help to explain them and make them clearer.

- *Feelings:* What were you thinking and feeling? Focus on your emotional state at the time, and consider how that affected your behaviour and your reactions to the behaviour of others. What might others have been thinking and feeling?

- *Evaluation:* What was good and bad? Identify your specific strengths and weaknesses.

- *Analysis:* What sense can you make of the situation? Use your knowledge of theory and practice to explain your own and others' behaviour.

- *Conclusion:* What else could you have done? What else could others have done? Consider alternative courses of action and their likely consequences.

- *Action plan for behaviour:* If it occurs again, what would you do? What changes in your/others' behaviour might be recommended?

- *Action plan for policy:* Are there any changes in overall policy that could be suggested/trialled?

(based on Moon 1999)

This is a detailed set of steps and it is impossible to fully engage with them if you do not make notes of your thoughts relating to every step. The best way to accomplish this is to keep a journal relating to your day-to-day practice. We are often presented with students who sigh, 'so I have to do a research report *and* keep a journal', to which our reply is that much of the material that is generated by the journal can be used as the basis of what goes into the research report; in this way a 'mad rush' to complete the write-up at the end from material whirling around in a tired brain, but nowhere on paper or PC file, can be avoided. Material that is collected within a journal can often also be used by practitioner students as the basis for several module assignments.

Starting a reflective journal and Continuing Professional Development portfolio

One of the most useful things to do, then, is to keep a reflective journal during your construction of your research project, which can then go on to form the first part of an ongoing Continuing Professional Development (CPD) portfolio. Initially, what you need to do is to produce a basic introduction to your setting and your role within it. This will need to be revised when inevitable changes occur (you move to a different role, move settings etc.). You should try to write an entry at least every three or four days, focusing on aspects of your work-based experience that caused you to reflect upon and develop your practice. Incidents that form the basis for your reflections may be positive, negative or neutral, and mundane, dramatic, funny or sad. You should not have to share your whole journal at any time (as this may inhibit the scope of your reflection), but it is useful from time to time to share edited extracts with fellow students, tutors and colleagues. *Do* make sure that your journal text is safely anonymised, particularly if you are storing it electronically – it is surprisingly easy to unwittingly stray outside data protection legislation if you use full, real names for colleagues, children and locations!

One of the things that you should find that emerges quite quickly from a journal where you are making regular entries is that your thoughts will tend to move in 'eddies', circling around particular practices or areas of your setting. In this way, you will begin to see potential topics for research.

When you first start to write your journal, aim to cover description/feelings/evaluation/analysis of the topics about which you are writing. As you get more practised (after approximately two or three weeks), you can back track to topics that keep emerging, making an attempt at an overall conclusion and action plan. You will no doubt find that part of this exercise comes up with the decision that 'more research is needed'. At this point, you are well on the way to seeing your research topic begin to emerge.

You don't have to go through this process alone. One of the ways to develop your skills of reflection is to carry out the conclusion and action planning process in small groups, discussing with your fellow students what conclusions you are intending to draw, and what the consequent implications for action planning might be.

> **Florentyna** writes in her journal: It was raining today, so Mrs B. said the children couldn't play outside. K. asked if they could put on the hooded overalls and wellies that we bought with some of the lottery grant money, but Mrs B. replied that they would 'catch their deaths'. I talked to some children standing by the window. Sam said, 'Why does rain go "splash", miss?' We talked about this for a while and then I opened the window so he could see the rain falling into a little puddle that had formed on the windowsill. Some other children came over to watch; one of them asked me what the word for 'splash' was in the other languages I knew, so we talked about that for a while and how all the words sounded similar to the noise that the rain made (e.g. German 'klatsch'). I felt sad that they had to stay inside.

> **Ellie** writes in her journal: Katie's key person was off today, so she followed several people in turn around the room, grizzling. All of them tried to pick her up and comfort her, and she calmed down a little every time, but it didn't last for very long, she was soon back again. When her mother came to collect her, she asked why Katie looked so flushed and miserable. I felt terrible about the whole thing.

> **Nick** writes in his journal: The TAs seem to bring much more enjoyment to literacy tasks than they do to numeracy. They are all good people and try their best to do whatever task they are asked to do well, but they just don't seem to engage in the numeracy as they do in the literacy. A particular worry I have is that they will communicate to the girls in the class that 'girls don't like maths' because they are all female and I am male. I've tried to start to address this through the questionnaire I gave out in the summer, but I'm not getting anywhere fast, and I'm beginning to get quite concerned.

Sunil writes: The boys were jigging around like jumping beans on the carpet when Mrs T. read them a story, but they really settled down to some great learning in the home corner garage I set up, which was brilliant.

Reflection point

How do you think each of these students might have extended these journal entries into evaluation and analysis? You could work on this task with some of your fellow students (don't be concerned if you find some of the entries more difficult to move forward than others, but do consider why this might be the case!). Then bring an example in from your own journal for discussion with one or two other students in your research group.

What are reliability/validity/representativeness/objectivity and why are they important?

You will consider these aspects far more deeply as you move on in your research, but you do need to consider the following as you put together your initial research proposal:

Reliability: Your research should be designed well enough for anyone carrying out the same method to get the same result. Something that produces the same result each time is reliable (for example, a car that starts every time you turn the key in the ignition is reliable). If you are designing a questionnaire you should design it so that the individuals you survey will have a similar understanding of the questions.

For example, a badly designed questionnaire looking at children's play preferences might not have considered that, once they are around two years old, boys and girls tend to respond to toys and games in quite a gendered fashion. If you do not make sure that you administer your questionnaire to the same number of parents of children of each sex, you might be falsely led to believe, for example, that the children in your setting are not particularly interested in football or dolls. In this case, of course, you would simply need to ask parents to state the gender of their child at the top of the questionnaire.

Validity: For a piece of research to be valid it needs to represent the topic fairly. For example, if you wanted to study the opinions of fathers relating to *current* practices in nursery education, and interviewed a sample of fathers without bothering to check the ages of their children, your results will not be valid – you have not actually studied what you thought you were studying.

This may seem to be a fairly obvious point, given a simple example of this nature, but beware, validity problems can emerge in a very subtle fashion. For example, if you are presuming that children who come from a background where other languages are spoken in their home all have English as a *second* language, you may be mistaken. You will need to check carefully what language the family principally uses to be sure. In cases where mother and father have different native languages you may find that the child is completely bilingual and there is no clear 'first' and 'second' language.

Representativeness: If you are going to claim that a group of people in society (e.g. fathers) have shown a particular set of opinions and/or behaviours you need to be sure that your results are representative. For example, what if the sample of fathers referred to above were all teachers? Do you think their opinions may not only relate to their parenting status but also to their professional knowledge of education?

The problem of objectivity: While this is a pressing problem in qualitative research it may also be an issue in some quantitative study with very narrow samples. Your tutor should help you to design questionnaire research so that the questions are asked in an objective fashion, but the problem of objectivity runs more deeply than this. For example, researchers may subconsciously look for samples who are likely to produce the results they expect to find, so when you are designing research you need to be aware of this and 'police' yourself in this way. Do not fear if you only have access to a small limited sample when you are carrying out research, however. As long as you are aware that your results are likely to be biased, and you can explain how and why in your report, there will be no problem. A large part of objectivity is being aware of the faults in your research process, and no research process, including those undertaken by professionals, is completely free of bias.

Reflection point

What should Nick, Sunil, Florentyna and Ellie do to ensure that they behave as objectively as possible? This is often a difficult aspect of carrying out research within one's own setting, and something that practitioner-researchers need to approach with great care.

Research ethics

Your research must also be undertaken in a morally considered fashion, making sure that you do not hurt, frighten or offend anyone while undertaking your research procedure. You must:

Receive informed consent to your research from both the setting and your intended participants before beginning your research. All participants and the setting leader should be asked to sign a formal permission slip, once what participation in your research will involve has been *fully* explained to them.

Be honest with your participants. You must be honest about what type of research you are doing and the type of data you are collecting so participants can give you *informed* consent to their participation. This raises particular problems if you are researching the behaviour of young children or carrying out observational research in a public place, and this will be further discussed in later chapters.

Be particularly careful if your participants are children. You *must* get written permission from parents to use a child under 18 as a research participant, and you should also get verbal permission from the child if they are over three to four years of age.

Protect your participants from harm. For example, you should not embarrass them by asking personal questions that make them feel uncomfortable, and you should not make them feel belittled, either within their own minds or in front of other people.

Protect your participants' privacy. When you create a questionnaire or undertake an observation, you should make sure that you only collect the details about your participants that you need for research purposes, usually their age and gender. You should never include personal information such as names and addresses linked to research data. It is also unethical to discuss the results from ongoing research in small venues such as classrooms and childcare settings, particularly when it relates to the participation of mutual colleagues, clients and acquaintances.

You should allow people to withdraw from your research. If people become uncomfortable when they are taking part in your research, you should allow them to withdraw immediately, with no further questions asked. This is particularly important if your participants are children.

What is the point of research ethics? The first point to make here is that it is common good manners to behave courteously towards your research participants. They are fellow human beings who have been kind enough to give up their time to help you with your research, answering questions, being watched as they go about their duties or filling in forms that they might not find particularly interesting. You should remember that you and other researchers would not be able to do your research without the participation of these people; if you behave unprofessionally and cause hurt or offence to them it might also mean that they and their families/friends will refuse to take part in social research in the future. It would only take one generation of researchers who are not properly taught research ethics to put social research in general in danger of cancellation due to widespread refusal to participate from the public.

> ## Reflection point
>
> What might Nick have already done that raises the problem of (very minor) harm? What must he do (or, more precisely, not do) now to avoid creating a more serious ethical violation?

Creating the research question

All research starts with a research question. As we have illustrated above, for the typical undergraduate Practitioner Research dissertation this needs to be a question that is based upon a discussion of the existing literature, that can be effectively investigated within a twelve-week period using a small participant sample located within one setting. In addition, the investigation should lead the researcher to draw some clear conclusions based on the relationship of the study findings to those of previous researchers, and consequent implications for practice within the relevant setting. This is what your tutor will be looking for in the early weeks of your Practitioner Research or Dissertation module. However, they cannot give you your research question; this is something that you must independently define with the tutor's help. Remember, a research question must be a very specific question, not a vague topic description. Consider, for example, how far Sunil's initial question, 'the importance of play for boys in a mixed age nursery/reception class', may be from fitting all the above requirements.

Reflection point

In collaboration with your fellow students, consider some potential research questions for Sunil, Florentyna, Ellie and Nick, and then debate whether/how far these will fit the requirements outlined above. Try to discuss problems as they emerge, 'tweaking' the question accordingly. Most research questions are crafted in this type of trial and error process.

What are the current debates arising from the increasing number of practitioner research projects/dissertations ongoing in Early Years settings?

Veteran practitioner-researcher Angela Anning proposes that the following should be deeply considered before embarking on a practitioner research project:

- The paramount importance of confidentiality in observing, listening to and reporting on the behaviours of young children and their parents.

- The need to understand the sensitive nature of using cameras and deciding what to write in field notes.

- The need to be very sensitive to the ways in which researchers attempt to engage in dialogue with very young children and in interview processes with Early Years workers.

- The impossibility of getting fully informed consent to be a research participant from a child under 7.

- The need to reflect on potential conflicts between a professional role serving the needs of children, families and communities and the researcher's role in 'objectifying' the objects of enquiry.

- The potential for the research processes to influence/change relationships with colleagues (for example, what if they express an opinion that is highly antithetical to your own? What if they exercise their right to withdraw from your research?).

- Are practitioners always able to be non-judgemental about practice in their setting (for example, when assessing a rota system that has previously caused the researcher a lot of personal inconvenience)?

- What will be the results of sharing your findings honestly with your colleagues? Might this create some issues within the setting, in certain circumstances?

Anning warns: 'The brutal fact is that your position as a professional gives you power over your community; but is it justifiable to use this power as a researcher as well, without serious thought and preparation?' (Anning 2010: 190). As such, it is not only your research grade that is dependent upon the thoroughness of your planning and preparation, but also the welfare of your participants. This is a huge responsibility, but also a challenge that people with the ambition to become senior practitioners should be willing to address, in the pursuit of developing a wide range of highly relevant personal and professional skills.

Conclusion

This chapter has introduced you to the basic concepts that you need to grasp in order to make a thoughtful, reflective start on the processes that you will need to enact in order to produce your dissertation or practitioner research assignment. The set of staged processes you will need to undertake makes the dissertation or practitioner research module somewhat different in style from other modules that you will study during your degree. Some of these processes will seem reasonably familiar, such as carrying out an amount of independent reading (although the fact that you largely set your own agenda for this may feel very different), while others may at first feel quite new and sometimes bewildering, for example paying attention to the set of issues that Anning raises in the section above, and using such ideas as a focus to ensure the ethical foundation of your research activities. All of this will need to be taken 'one bite at a time', as we advise on page 2, with (of course) the support of your tutor. In order to have the necessary time available over the period of the module delivery (particularly if you are also coping with a substantial work or work placement schedule), you will need to manage your time extremely carefully. As such, the very first process that you will need to begin as soon as possible is independent reading around the topic that you have picked as the focus of your dissertation. We will therefore immediately address this by helping you to make the most of the library resources that are available to you; this is the focus of the next chapter.

References

Anning, A. (2010) 'Research' in early years settings, a pause for thought, *Early Years: An International Journal of Research and Development*, 30 (2): 189–91.

Moon, J. (1999) *Learning Journals: A handbook for Academics, Students and Professional Development*, London: Routledge Falmer.

Chapter 2
Reading for research: efficient use of your access to an academic library

Rónán O'Beirne and Pam Jarvis

Introduction

While everyone taking a higher education qualification should have sound basic literacy skills, students do not always realise that 'just reading' is not the same as 'reading for research'. This chapter will comprehensively introduce this concept, through its coverage of the following topics:

- Introduction to using the internet for research
- Literature searching, including a comprehensive guide to literature searches on the internet, with a particular focus on using online university e-journal access
- Recording for referencing
- Narrowing your focus
- Deciding on a 'working title'
- Reading strategically
- Avoiding plagiarism

It will err on the side of including 'complete' information to support the full range of readers, some of whom may have rather skimped on the development of their library skills up to this point of their studies!

Finding and using information to support research

The first chapter of this book deals with how to initially define your research question and make a start on your Early Years research project; in this chapter we would like to consider the information management aspect of research, without which you cannot make an effective start. By this we mean the strategy you will employ to retrieve, collect, manage, arrange, organise, reflect upon and, eventually, present information about your research.

Before you can begin to organise your thoughts about the subject area into which you have chosen to carry out your research, you first of all need to have an overview of the territory. Although this is fairly straightforward it can sometimes seem like 'extra work' to look at the wider picture when perhaps you have identified a narrower area for your inquiry. However, in order to retrieve useful information you will need to know what is relevant and what is current; the only way to know this is to have that overview, which in turn outlines the boundaries of your topic and reveals what is on the edges of your area of interest.

Sunil came away from his introduction to the library discouraged and confused. There seemed to be so many places to look for information. He had thought he could get by with Google and the World Wide Web. What did they mean: 'never use Wikipedia because the information is not peer reviewed'? Good old Wikipedia had been the main source of information for his Foundation Degree assignments. He slumped into his car and turned on Radio Five sports.

Nick found his introduction to the library quite fascinating. Although he had been introduced to library skills in his first degree, he had never been properly introduced to the Dewey Decimal cataloguing system before. He put the library exercises sheet carefully into his bag, determining to arrive at college early next week, in order to practise his searching skills.

Florentyna found some of the library skills advice quite familiar. She had been taught how to use an academic library during her first degree in her own country and much of the cataloguing was the same. The librarian had not covered searches using languages other than English, and she wanted to see if she could find some of Vygotsky's writings on play in the original Russian. She made a note to email the librarian.

Ellie walked slowly away from the library feeling dazed and confused. She had prepared to read a lot of books to underpin her dissertation literature review; now she realised that much of the information was to be found online, and while she used the nursery computer for the necessary record keeping, typed up her assignments on 'Word' and had made a stab at 'PowerPoint' now and again for presentations to staff and parents, she did not feel 'at home' in the online world. Yet another steep learning curve to negotiate, she sighed to herself.

Reflection point

Imagine that each of these students confides their thoughts and feelings to you. How would you advise them to deal with potential issues arising?

In recent times much has been written about the skills needed to gain an overview of, and indeed to zoom in and target, a specific area of research. A good deal of what has been written has focused on the way information, and the means of accessing information, has changed dramatically with the introduction of computers. The increase in the amount of information has been significant and our focus here will be on how technology can be used as a tool to assist research. In this chapter, we will look at how researchers can find the right information by using the right tools and how this information can be used to support research. To open, it is necessary to assess the benefits of different types of information and different formats of information. We will then explore the use of library-based resources such as books and electronic journals before moving on to the use of networked resources such as the World Wide Web. To conclude the chapter we will identify the common pitfalls encountered when using information sources, such as copyright infringement and plagiarism, and will look at how these pitfalls can be avoided.

One thing that needs to be stressed is that in order to develop your own research you absolutely need to read; and you need to read in a proactive 'academic' way right from day one. Many of us find we are too busy or too easily distracted to read effectively, but it is not possible to carry out an acceptable standard of research without making a full commitment to reading. The good news, however, is that you don't necessarily need to read everything. In fact, what really matters is that you read the right things. You need to develop a knack of reading the important material thoroughly while giving the less important material a cursory skim read. In other words you need to be strategic in your approach.

It is important to try to get an overview of the literature by posing some key questions at the outset. What you will be investigating will be a subset of a wider subject within the overall field of Early Years, Childcare and Education. The better the picture you can give of your context, the easier it will be for you to draw your audience into your research. It allows your audience to position your research effectively within the overall field and perhaps more widely. You are looking therefore, through your reading of the literature, to identify key writers who have made a significant contribution to the wider theme. You should, as a rule, start with the general and work towards the specific. You will need to think carefully about the balance of your literature review. Obviously if you write too much about a general background you limit the space you need for the specific aspects of your research. On the other hand if you dive straight into specifics you risk leaving your readers wondering about the background. It is important to get these in the right proportion; this balance can only be achieved through writing a number of drafts. So, as well as needing to read, you also need to be prepared to write! (See Chapter 3.)

Nick turns off his desk light at 1.30 am and runs his hand through his hair (rapidly thinning, he thinks wryly to himself). He looks at the huge pile of books and printed articles on the desk. He has been working on his literature review for a fortnight now. His library searches have turned up a huge amount of information and he is trying to encompass it all in his 3000-word literature review. His tutor has told him to 'be selective', but Nick does not really see what she means. The next day, he speaks to his tutor again, and after skim reading Nick's latest draft, she advises him to separate the literature into 'themes' and write a short piece on each one before attempting to relate them to his research question. This should indicate which can stay and which need to go, and from this point he should be able to make more informed decisions about future directions in his reading.

Ellie sits in her living room surrounded by books and printed journal articles. She has been reading for the past fortnight, but she has not yet written anything. Nothing seems *directly* relevant to the project that she so meticulously planned. She shares her problem with her tutor the following day, and is advised to make summary notes on each source, file them carefully and then revisit them with her research question in mind. Ellie cannot see how this will be relevant, but begins to make notes during her next reading session.

Florentyna has found some very interesting German sources on Forest Schools. She tells her colleague about them the following day, and is concerned to see that her colleague clearly thinks that how things are done 'on the continent' is nothing much to do with the English Children's Centre in which they both work. Florentyna's tutor advises her to read some material on cultural differences in childcare.

Sunil sees his tutor in the corridor a fortnight after his library introduction. He turns to walk in the opposite direction, but too late, the tutor has seen him. She walks over and asks in a friendly tone how the reading is going. 'Fine', answers Sunil, while thinking, 'I *really* must make a start tonight'.

Reflection point

What problems do you think each student may be having at the moment? How do you think each one could begin to address these?

Your identification of key writers in your area of research will most likely be straightforward; you will probably identify such writers from course textbooks or from your required reading list. These writers will have written key texts, either books or articles in specialist journals. A good starting point would be to write down all the key players and try to assign some sequence to the timing of their writing by using dates of publication.

After identifying key writers, try to pick up on the terms that are being used. Don't assume that common terms, or terms with which you are familiar in another context, will have the same definition across all the literature; much of the debate around topics will focus on how definitions of terms are assigned and used. It is also useful to try to understand any cultural differences. If, like Florentyna, you are looking at literature from a range of geographical locations remember that translation always creates the potential for misinterpretation, whether you are managing the translation yourself, like Florentyna, or reading material that has been translated into English by the author. After you have identified writers and key terms within the literature you should begin to look for seminal or 'key' pieces of research. These could be characterised by frequent citation in the literature and might form research milestones in the development of the topic. Moreover they are often the foundations or impetus for further investigations. Tutors can help you with this task, but do not expect them to do it for you! By pulling together these elements you should begin to grasp the key concepts of the topic.

Ellie feels as though she is on the brink of giving up. She started a project with a focus on the role of the key person in Early Years in order to introduce exemplary practice into her setting. But on reading as much as she can find about attachment theory, she begins to realise that it is impossible for a key person to be present 100 per cent of the time for a child being cared for in a commercial childcare setting. She discusses this with her tutor. Her tutor asks whether, with the knowledge she has gained, Ellie can now aim for the best practice possible from a position that is more informed than she could have done three months ago. Ellie thinks about this for a moment and agrees that yes, that is probably the case. So, her tutor asks, could she put together a project to improve practice, if this consisted of making and testing a series of minor changes in the setting? Ellie thinks that this would be possible. The tutor suggests that Ellie create her literature review around this concept, in terms of improving practice along the lines of the underpinning theory. Ellie goes away feeling rather better about her project than she has previously.

Nick is also in a phase of frustration. He started this project with the aim of improving his Teaching Assistants' (TAs') mathematical skills, and thought that this would immediately translate into improved practice in the classroom, but now he is beginning to realise that this was a huge over-simplification of the situation. His tutor asks him if the support staff *really* do not have the mathematical competence to understand the level of mathematical learning undertaken by the children in his class. Nick considers this and comes to the conclusion that this is unlikely to be the case. His tutor asks him if the confidence and enjoyment of the adults may have more to do with the issues that Nick has previously identified. She suggests that Nick observe his TAs over the following week to consider this possibility.

Florentyna is beginning to compare the Early Years guidelines from several European countries. Her tutor asks her to consider the level of adult control exerted over the learning process within each nation and how this might reflect upon the confidence with which Early Years practitioners engage in Forest School practices. Florentyna feels that she is on the brink of the analytical approach that she wants to take to her project.

The challenge of finding 'secondary source' information

A good starting point is for you to consider what your information needs are for a particular assignment or project. Consider, for example, how you get information on a day-to-day basis. A good way to begin to understand information gathering is to place yourself at the centre of your own information world; by doing this you can have a clearer sense of orientation. First-hand information, existing within your local world, contains information, ideas and opinions that you understand or of which you have experience. Academic researchers call this 'anecdotal information' – information we gather from anecdotes about our own everyday lives, but have never systematically tested. You will receive this type of information through your involvement with your local communities at home, work and college. Second-hand information might be considered to be that information that you receive via the radio or TV or that you read in a book or magazine or through everyday internet browsing. A tiny amount of this information may be about interesting new results from academic studies, but the vast majority will be highly anecdotal, for example 'news' stories about the behaviour of very highly paid media stars, or a particularly nasty murder.

Now try to expand this further to include information you can gather from a wider circle of sources, for example the wider internet, or reference books. Notice that the formats can change, sometimes in print and sometimes electronic. There are many different types of information and there are different formats of information:

- TV news, e.g. the latest position on the economy or an emerging perspective, e.g. government support for families, or discipline in schools.

- Ideas that you or others may have about a certain topic, e.g. Facebook forum.

- Opinions, 'think' pieces or morally held beliefs, e.g. a newspaper editorial.

- Handbooks, guidebooks, bus timetables, telephone directories, an Early Years statutory guidance document.

- Graphical information, e.g. maps, photographs, satellite navigation systems, diagrams of care/education processes.

- Statistics and figures, e.g. rising or falling birth rates and their impact on nursery and school admissions, now and in the future.

- Historical accounts, time-lines, artifacts in museums, rare film footage, e.g. of teachers and children in the early twentieth century.

- Human interest stories in newspapers or popular magazines, e.g. children/ families with rare special needs or in unusual circumstances.

- Support, advice or guidance, e.g. human (and increasingly IT-based) interventions to aid decision making, e.g. choice of intervention programmes for children with particular special needs such as hearing impairment or dyslexia.

- Technical information, chemical transport symbols, architectural drawings, instructions about medicine doses and effects.

- Legal information, terms of use, acceptable practice policies, contracts of employment.

- Research results, e.g. reports relating to effects emerging from a particular teaching or care method.

- Theories, views and debates in journals, books and websites.

Using your academic library

When searching for information for your academic writing you must remember to distinguish between **peer reviewed** and **non-peer reviewed** papers. Peer reviewed papers carry much more 'weight' in the academic world than non-peer reviewed. This is because the process of peer review involves several people who are respected within their academic discipline agreeing that a paper is a scholarly contribution to extend the field of knowledge in a non-biased way, and worthy of publication. If the paper concerned is reporting research, this means that the reviewers feel that the research was rigorously and ethically carried out, or if it is a review of the literature in a particular area, this means that the reviewers judge that the author has constructed a logical debate and conclusion that is of value to others within the profession. A paper or article that is non-peer reviewed will be purely the opinion of the person who wrote it, so using such material within an academic assignment means that you are relying on the opinion of an author to be of merit without first having to pass the test of a peer review. It is therefore not advisable to rest the body of your evidence for a particular argument on non-peer reviewed sources such as Wikipedia. Blogs and other pages on the World Wide Web can also be less than reliable or accurate and often that 'scholarly extension of the body of knowledge' is missing. You should beware content that has been posted by one person to expound their individual, anecdotal views upon a topic. Unfortunately there are literally millions of such pages to be found on the web relating to childcare and education.

Your university or college academic library is the first place to look for reliable, peer reviewed information. Most academic libraries provide a wide range of printed materials in the form of books and journals. Books are stored on shelves and there is a classification system that means all books that are similar in content, i.e. have the same subject, are shelved near each other. This helps people to find books that are related to each other by subject. One of the popular systems of classification is known as the Dewey Decimal Classification system (DDC). The Main Classes are divided into the following numbers which are translated into labels on the spines of the book; books on library shelves have their numbers in increasing order and always run from left to right. Here are the ten highest level classifications for Dewey:

000 Computer science, information & general works

100 Philosophy & psychology

200 Religion

300 Social sciences

400 Language

500 Science

600 Technology

700 Arts & recreation

800 Literature

900 History & geography

Social Science, you can see, is given the number 300. Within this there are ten sub-divisions:

300 Social sciences, sociology & anthropology

310 Statistics

320 Political science

330 Economics

340 Law

350 Public administration & military science

360 Social problems & social services

370 Education

380 Commerce, communications & transportation

390 Customs, etiquette & folklore

Sub-divisions of Education are as follows:

371 Schools & their activities; special education

372 Elementary education

373 Secondary education

374 Adult education

375 Curricula

376 [Unassigned]

377 [Unassigned]

378 Higher education

379 Public policy issues in education

The hierarchy of Dewey is the arrangement of the system from general to specific. The length of the notation and the corresponding depth of indention of the heading usually indicate the degree of specificity of a class. It is always advisable to work from the general to the specific when searching. The display of books in a library allows you to browse particular areas that have related content. But do remember that if you were looking at, for example, the use of poetry in primary schools you would look at shelf number 372.64 but may also find relevant material in, for example, 821.08 which is the shelf number for poetry.

When considering books you should remember that it takes from about nine months to two years to publish a book. So in many cases the treatment of highly topical issues may be out-of-date by the time they appear in print in a book. To balance this you should be aware that books often offer a more in-depth and rounded treatment of issues than journal articles, simply because a book can examine issues at greater length and, within the more extensive writing process required for a book, the authors have had more time to reflect. Electronic books or e-books are often versions of print editions made available in a digital format and accessible via a network. This being the case, it is not necessarily true that their content is more up-to-date than print versions. Material and content retrieved from websites may be more current but may lack an element of reflection or, as outlined above, may not have the same level of academic rigour. There are issues with both approaches and it is worth bearing these in mind when considering the wider implications of your research strategy.

The library catalogue

The library catalogue is the key tool for finding information in the library collection. Traditionally the catalogue was a paper-based list of all the books that were physically stored in that library, but nowadays practically all catalogues are electronic and can be searched through a graphical user interface on a computer screen; this means that you can check your library's catalogue over the internet.

It is important to realise that in most libraries the complete book stock is rarely displayed on the open access shelves; there are usually a lot of print items stored away behind the scenes. For this reason it is important to get into the habit of using the library catalogue as the first port of call. Libraries usually have special collections of material, sometimes fragile and/or of high value; this material is rarely on open display but will always be catalogued. Also, as many libraries replace their printed books with e-books it becomes even more important to use the catalogue effectively. Most libraries will have special arrangements to exchange items and extend borrowing rights with other libraries; the best way to find out about this is to ask the librarian.

It is also worth mentioning WorldCat (www.worldcat.org), which is a catalogue of catalogues worldwide: 'the world's largest network of library content and services. WorldCat libraries are dedicated to providing access to their resources on the web, where most people start their search for information' (WorldCat, online). WorldCat is useful for checking bibliographic details and locating copies in nearby libraries; it can also be used to generate citations using a number of referencing standards.

There are two main ways of searching an online catalogue, and these are similar to the two main ways of searching the shelves of the library. The first way is to 'browse'; so just like looking through the bookshelves under a particular classification number or subject heading, it is possible to browse through a catalogue using a particular subject classification. This way you will find material that is related to a specific topic.

The second way to search is for a known item. You want to find a particular book so you search for it by typing the title into the catalogue and the system retrieves the full details of the title and tells you where it can be found in the library; this type of search is called a 'known item' search. It is possible to combine both search approaches: to look for a particular author (known item) and then to search through (browse) that author's writings until you find something interesting. A half-way point is to use a keyword search. This involves choosing keywords that might appear in the title of the book you are looking for or might have been assigned by the compilers of the catalogue. Through the search interface you can select various different aspects to your search and this will then return results on a separate results screen. This principle is true for library catalogues, electronic databases and World Wide Web search engines like Google.

In all systems there is an inverse relation between recall and precision that needs to be understood. If you understand this relation you will be able to find things more effectively, so take time to consider this.

Armstrong and Large (2001: 14) note:

> **Recall** is a measure of effectiveness in retrieving **all** the sought information in a database – that is, in search comprehensiveness. A search would achieve perfect recall if every single record that should be found in relation to a specific query is indeed traced. It is normally expressed in proportional terms.

Precision, however, assesses the accuracy of the search in terms of its relevancy. What tends to happen is that as recall is increased, proportionally there are fewer relevant hits returned, i.e. as precision is increased, recall is decreased and vice versa. It is very important to think about this relationship and to understand it fully because all electronic retrieval systems – the library catalogue, indexes to journals and Google – operate on this rule.

Sunil

. . . wants to find articles that give him an overview of his subject. His topic is 'boys learning through play', but when it comes to searching he does not really know where to start. He has typed *boys learning through play* into Google and it has returned a staggering 104 million results. Harry, the Education Faculty librarian in the college library, suggests that Sunil needs to break his search down into stages. If the key term is 'boys learning through play' Harry suggests that if these words are kept together and enclosed in inverted commas like this, 'boys learning through play', then search systems will treat this as a phrase. Also, Harry asks Sunil if he is interested in this topic from any particular angle (for example, what timeframe – during the last three or three hundred years or since 1950)? Also, is Sunil interested in a particular location? – for example, as extensive as the whole USA, or as specific as one part of a city – upper-Manhattan, the north bank of the Seine or South London? Or, like most of the other students Harry has seen in the past couple of weeks, does Sunil require some information that is broadly based within the UK/other English-speaking countries, and some that is specific to schools working to the English National Curriculum? Harry additionally enquires what type of material Sunil hopes to find, for example conference proceedings, books, journal articles.

Sunil begins to realise that he needs to think very carefully about the scope of his research. With little precision Sunil will have huge recall, resulting in too many search results which will swamp him rather than give him an overview. Harry suggests to Sunil that he could also think about other words that could be used in his search, words that have a similar meaning. Finally the 'syntax' of the search should be carefully considered because combining terms and restricting certain words can increase precision. Harry then takes Sunil through some quite brief but informative library 'demos' giving practical illustrations of what can be achieved by academic resource library searches, which Sunil missed due to leaving early on one of his induction days.

Reflection point

Sunil walks away thinking that, although it was a lot to take in, he was glad that he had finally plucked up the courage to speak to Harry. At times he had feared that the college librarians might be starchy or superior, remembering the librarian at school glaring over her glasses at him and making loud 'shushing' noises! But Harry had not been a bit like that; he had been very helpful, and spoke to Sunil in a way that suggested that such questions were an everyday part of his job. Even better, Sunil now feels confident to start using his online access to the college library through his student webpage, and will be able to work on literature sourcing at any time of the day or night, very convenient to a 'night owl' like himself.

Why not get to know the 'Harry' allocated to Education/Early Years in your college library if you are not already acquainted with him or her? It is one of the most useful things you can do at the beginning of your dissertation module.

Journals

Research papers and conference papers often surface as journal articles – remember there is a time lag between time of submissions by the authors to the journal and the journal actually publishing the article; this can be as long as a year to eighteen months. It is always a good idea to look at a number of issues of a particular journal before citing one of its articles; this is because often a paper may be challenged in a later issue of the journal. It is therefore good practice to skim read previous and later issues of the journal. If we think about finding the right information in articles in journals and those journals dispersed all over the place, some in print in the library, some electronic on the web, the difficulty we might have in finding the right article in the right journal might seem like finding a needle in a haystack. However, the task of finding the right information in the right journal is made easier because almost all professional and scholarly journals have indexing systems to help their readers to find articles.

Here are some of the most important index systems to journals that will be particularly relevant to your studies:

- The **British Education Index:** an independent subject and author index to the contents of significant education journals published in the UK.

- **ERIC** – the **Education Resources Information Center:** an online digital library of education research and information.

- **Social Sciences Citation Index®:** accessed via **Web of Science®**, provides researchers, administrators, faculty and students with quick, powerful access to the bibliographic and citation information they need to find research data, analyse trends, journals and researchers, and share their findings.

- **Google Scholar:** provides a simple way to search broadly for scholarly literature. It is a portal to resources across many disciplines and sources: articles, theses, books, abstracts and court opinions, from academic publishers, professional societies, online repositories, universities and other websites.

- **General search engines:** A search engine harvests information about websites on the internet and creates a very large index of terms and associated hyperlinks. When someone queries (searches) a search engine they are in fact looking up the index. Because the engine is constantly harvesting and generating index terms, **recall** can be very high; however, as outlined above, **precision** is usually poor unless you use some of the more advanced features of search engines. It is important that you familiarise yourself with these features as Sunil did, and your faculty librarian, like his, will be pleased to demonstrate the advanced features of any or several search engine(s).

Another resource of immense value worth exploring for useful material although not restricted to the field of education is **The Directory of Open Access Journals**, which is a listing of open access journals, available without subscription fees, in all fields of knowledge.

A further approach to keeping tabs on journal publications is to make use of the tables of contents of collections of journals. **Zetoc** provides access to the British Library's Electronic Table of Contents of around 20,000 current journals and around 16,000 conference proceedings published per year. The database covers 1993 to date, and is updated on a daily basis. It includes an email alerting service, to enable you to keep up-to-date with relevant new articles and papers in your topic area. Zetoc itself provides access to the table of contents rather than the full text. However, once you have found an article of interest, the full record page provides three links to help you access the full text.

Using social media and networks to support research

With the increased use of social media and social networking it is possible to take different approaches to your research. First of all the process of researching can be seen to have a social dimension with the use of Web 2.0 technologies. This means that researchers (and that includes you as a dissertation module student) can communicate and share their research activity online. There are obvious benefits in this social approach as for example **Method Space**, where the emphasis is on research methods, provides resources and a forum for discussion among researchers. **Research Gate**, primarily focused on scientific research, has a growing representation in the social sciences and education disciplines. More generally communication through blogs such as: **Blogger, LiveJournal, TypePad** and **WordPress**, and through Microblogging: **Twitter, Yammer** and **Google Plus** provides the opportunity for those involved in research projects or in a similar field to set up a space where their communication is both facilitated and recorded. Networks such as **Facebook, LinkedIn** and to a lesser extent **MySpace** can be used to generate communities of shared interest and practice. Communication is of immense value in today's research environments and getting linked into a relevant network is of huge importance.

Managing content on the web has changed in recent years, so in contrast to the task of searching out information, covered earlier in this chapter, the task of organising webpages, links, documents, slideshows, videos and references that you have found on the web can be quite a challenge. Aggregators such as

Google reader, **Netvibes**, **Pageflakes** and more recently **Flipboard** are useful ways to manage your content. Social bookmarking introduces the concept of collaboration where the real benefits of 'social' networking can be seen. Social bookmarking, using tools such as **Delicious**, **Diigo** and **BibSonomy**, allows you to assign your own 'tags' or index terms to content that you have retrieved online. You build your own set of references, and can organise this content in a number of ways. In a similar way social bibliography services such as **CiteULike** and **Mendeley** allow you to organise and share citation information which can be useful. This is of course a very brief introduction, so, again, do consult your college librarian for further information.

If you do use these types of services and become engaged in social networking then you should do so in a cautious way. There can be issues around the quality and timeliness of material and around intellectual property rights. You should also be mindful of your reputation and that of your institution; as a student, and as a professional practitioner, you should be aware that something that has been written in one of these many social networks cannot be easily removed, and may still be found by someone putting your name into Google for many years to come. All the warnings that have surfaced about use of 'Facebook' without consideration of your personal privacy apply here, with equal respect to your professional reputation – something that teachers and Early Years practitioners should guard very carefully, in this world of instant online accusation and counter-accusation. See, for example, *My Twitter row with Stephen Fry* (Yiannopolous 2010).

Plagiarism

It is worth mentioning at the close of this chapter that plagiarism can be a problem for many students when they are faced with producing a significant body of independent writing. Plagiarism is dealt with so harshly because it is at root a type of theft – stealing others' ideas and phrasing to present them as your own. While some students do cheat and are guilty of collusion, by far the most common form of plagiarism detected is poorly addressed or absent referencing. It is possible to plagiarise accidentally if you get into the bad habit of downloading chunks of material from internet sources and dropping them into your notes to 'work on' later. The potential then arises for the student to forget to do this work/add the necessary reference, and subsequently they will submit an assignment with one or more plagiarised sections. The moral to this story is: never copy and paste into the file that contains your assignment text;

create another file called 'quotes' (or similar) and store any copy and paste material here.

While some suggest that the ease with which students can copy and paste material is the reason for the higher level of plagiarism, others suggest that increased effectiveness in plagiarism detection through electronic systems (such as 'Copycatch' and 'Turnitin') and the greater likelihood of being detected have exposed a problem that has always been there. Either way advanced software used by many institutions is catching and punishing plagiarism. Most institutions will have a system through which students can check their final copy assignment for plagiarism; the report you get will be identical to the one the tutor sees when they open your submitted work to mark. It is advisable to check every assignment in this way before submission; better safe than sorry. Your tutor/college librarian can help you understand the report, and which aspects of it should be given the greatest attention.

Managing the way you insert quotes from other authors is extremely important. You absolutely must ensure that you maintain a meticulous system for recording the references you make. If you paraphrase an author you also need to provide a reference. When you quote you need to be careful that you quote directly and accurately and that you attribute that quoted text to the original author. Never 'quote from a quote' unless there is a compelling reason to do so. Additionally, never ever put a quote in your text without a full reference, and always complete the reference in full at the time you make the quote – if you leave your bibliography/reference list until the end it will lead to confusion and error.

Please be aware that there are a number of accepted referencing systems, and you will need to find out which one is used by your institution. However, your quest is not finished at this point, as it is not uncommon for particular institutions to have their own variant on a standard. Most institutions have their own referencing guide; make sure that you use this carefully. (See Chapter 9 for more on referencing.)

The key point that we would like to emphasise as this chapter comes to a close is that faculty librarians are a hugely valuable resource for a dissertation student. They can provide ongoing help in sourcing materials, both physical and online, and by so doing save you from hours of fruitless searching and the frustration that this creates. Librarians are employed to fill an important role within their institution because their training has prepared them to know everything that you need to know about sourcing literature for your dissertation, and they will only be too pleased to help.

Conclusion

This chapter has introduced you to the basic concepts that you need to grasp to make the maximum use of a modern academic library; your college librarian can no doubt fill in the details from this point onwards. While some of the skills that students need to develop, such as an understanding of the process of cataloguing resources and the ability to swiftly skim-read abstracts/catalogue entries in order to select the most relevant books and articles, are perennial, some of the processes of storing and recording academic literature are changing rapidly, as are the media on which resources are accessed. It is likely that during the lifetime of this book new 'apps' will be developed for smartphones and their technological successors that will revolutionise the way that students use academic libraries. It is also possible that, just as at the turn of the twentieth century a new generation took an interest in 'retro' media such as vinyl records in a world of CDs and track downloads, there may at some point be a renewed surge of interest in paper-based resources. In such a flexible environment, the writers of this book urge you to focus principally upon developing the core literature searching skill of reading quickly but accurately, regardless of the medium upon which you are accessing a document – this only develops through focused practice. Developing academic literature searching skills is rather like learning to ride a bicycle: you have to have some independent experience of the mistakes that lead you to 'fall off' before you can learn how to balance yourself properly! The next chapter will assume that you have emerged from the preliminary 'reading research' stage, and will engage with you at the point of beginning to craft the very first section of the report that you will focus on: the literature review.

References

Armstrong, C.J. and Large, A. (2001) *Manual of online search strategies 3, Humanities and social sciences*, Aldershot: Gower.

MethodSpace (2011) MethodSpace home page: http://www.methodspace.com/ [accessed 4 November 2011].

ResearchGate (2011) ResearchGate front page: http://www.researchgate.net/ [accessed 4 November 2011].

WorldCat (2011) What is WorldCat?: http://www.worldcat.org/whatis/default.jsp [accessed 4 November 2011].

Yiannopolous, M. (2010) My Twitter row with Stephen Fry: http://www.telegraph.co.uk/comment/personal-view/8137164/My-Twitter-row-with-Stephen-Fry.html [accessed 28 October 2011].

Chapter 3
The literature review and sectioning the project write-up

Pam Jarvis

Introduction

This chapter will consider the literature review in detail. It assumes that, following Chapter 2, you have selected a body of literature to review, and that you are reading through this in an academic fashion, which includes taking notes on its contents. This does not mean, however, you do not need to return to the library. Throughout the period of your research, you should always be prepared to follow up an interesting reference, and to keep up-to-date with literature alerts such as Zetoc (see Chapter 2) in order to follow up any interesting leads.

Our students now all have a title for their projects, and three have working research questions, as follows:

Ellie has stuck with her idea of studying the role of the key person in Early Years. Her title is 'Attachment Theory and the Role of the Key Person' and her working research question for her dissertation is: 'To what extent can the key person address young children's need for a bonded relationship within a collective care setting?'

Nick has developed his idea relating to supporting mathematical learning in the Early Years. He has discussed his focus on the role of support workers with his tutor several times, and has now come to the conclusion that focusing on their role may not be particularly productive in terms of learning about his own practice (given that he is addressing a practitioner research module), and that he will focus more generally on developing activities and resources for children in the Early Years who may already be on the way to subscribing to the stereotype that 'maths is hard'. His title is 'Making Maths Fun in the Early Years', and his working research question is: 'How can mathematical activities be made more relevant to children's interests in a flexible and individualised way?'

Florentyna has decided, despite some discouraging responses from her colleagues, to stay with her idea of studying the development of outdoor play in her setting, using concepts from the Forest Schools movement. She is aware that this might be difficult within an urban English setting, but the management have agreed that she can take charge of a small, neglected grassed area at the back of the setting, and develop this into a safe area for the children to play in a natural environment. The emphasis in this agreement was upon 'safe', and Florentyna is avidly reading English and American literature on the topic of 'risky play'. Her title is 'Bringing Forest School Practice to the City' and her working research question is: 'What activities can bring the practice of the Forest School to an urban English Early Years setting?'

Sunil has developed a focus upon learning through play for boys in nursery and reception after several long conversations with his tutor. Initially he struggled with the extent of this topic in terms of the numerous areas of learning identified within the current Early Years practice guidance documents. His title is

▶

'Boys Learning Through Play in the Early Years', but he does not yet have a fully formed research question. His tutor suggests that he ask one of the teachers he works with about a useful project that he might take on board to develop an area of learning through play focusing on the boys. The nursery teacher shows huge interest in this, and suggests that Sunil develop some pre-literacy activities for boys that emphasise the uses of reading in activities that they enjoy, in particular considering how this can encompass both the indoor and outdoor environments. A couple of days later, Sunil's nephew sits watching 'Thomas the Tank Engine' at breakfast time. This leads Sunil to reflect that his 'guys' love playing 'trains' in the outdoor area. As Henry, the number 3 green engine, pulls into a station, Sunil looks at the station name sign on the screen and begins to formulate an idea....

Why review the literature?

In summary, this can be simply defined as follows:

- To gain knowledge of the subject area
- To find out where there may be gaps in theoretical/empirical knowledge
- To rethink/refocus your research question
- To discover how others have approached research in this area
- To be able to compare your own research findings with those of others.

Those who attempt to do research without first creating a literature review are doing what is colloquially referred to as 'reinventing the wheel'. Given that study within the social sciences has been formally ongoing for the past 250 years, it is likely that someone starting without first examining the relevant literature will simply repeat what others have done before them, and, more problematically, start from a position that has long ago been passed, additionally clouding their activities with a wholly anecdotal perspective (see Chapter 2). Through speech and later writing, the sum of human achievement became cumulative across generations; in the classical quote that derives from Greek and Latin scholars, in our research activities we 'stand upon the shoulders of giants'. Students of all disciplines taking first degrees are expected to learn how this process works and, in their second and third years, to produce independent research following the conventions of academic enquiry, engaging with the work of previous researchers and producing their own research within this ancient, international convention of scholarly research. There is no requirement for an undergraduate student to produce *new* knowledge (this is the focus of the postgraduate PhD), but there is a requirement to demonstrate understanding of the body of academic knowledge underpinning the area of research in which the project is undertaken, and to then test these ideas on the basis of the knowledge that has been constructed in the process of carrying out the literature review.

Nick

. . . rifles through his file of notes. He has done what his tutor suggested and separated his notes into sections, which he has re-organised several times. Although it has been hard work, and quite lonely sometimes, reading from books and his laptop, sitting in his living room late at night, he is beginning to consider how much he has learnt, and how this has changed his perspective on teaching, very much for the better, he reflects. Prior to undertaking his research, he frequently became quite exasperated with his TAs, who (he had perceived) just would not do exactly as he told them when they were set to a numeracy activity. Now he begins to understand that he was maybe presuming that both the TAs and the children thought about mathematical concepts in the same ways that he does, which he now realises is highly unlikely, given that he has a maths 'A' level, studied many mathematically related modules in his first degree and routinely used mathematically related skills in his previous employment. He turns his PC on to search for an article he downloaded that day on practical maths in play for children aged 3-5 years.

What is required in the undergraduate literature review?

In simple summary, the student is required to demonstrate that they have done the following:

- Identified relevant theory and research data
- Understood the theory and research data that they have cited
- Offered some considered evaluation of the sources that they have cited
- Successfully related the sources cited to the research that they intend to carry out.

A common mistake that students make in putting together a literature review is the assumption that they are expected to cram everything they know about a particular topic into 2000-2500 words (or whatever the word limit is for the assignment in question). This could not be further from the truth. What is expected is an outline of the *relevant* literature, organised in *relevant* themes (see below). What is relevant will depend on the specific research question.

This may lead some to say, 'But I can't find anything that is completely relevant to my research question.' This is when you need to refer back to your tutor. In some cases, you may be perceiving too narrow a relevance. For example, Ellie will not only need to access literature directly relating to the role of the key person, but also more general literature about attachment theory, in particular literature relating to the study of 'multiple attachments'. In other cases, the research question may be at fault; typically this may be a problem with being too general or too narrow. If this is the case, it will need to be re-crafted with the help of your tutor. While students may perceive this process as fiddly and nerve-wracking, it is a crucial step in developing generic graduate skills that allow one to become discerning about the uses and limitations of research, and to understand why tabloid headlines proposing 'miracle cures' or 'pure evil' people are not of use in terms of reflecting reality.

I have often had students tell me, 'But I read so much more than I actually use in the literature review . . . it is such a waste of time.' My response to this is that undergraduate research students are rather like the princess in the old fairy tale – in order to find the material that they need (and to develop their research skills) there is no getting away from the fact that they will 'have to kiss a lot of frogs to find Prince Charming', and that this is a process that all would-be researchers have to go through!

Based on: www.parachutingfish.com/2008/10/kissing-frogs/

Sunil

. . . walks away from his tutorial with a research question that his tutor has reassured him will do on a 'working' basis: 'What activities might be successful in encouraging boys to engage in pre-literacy tasks?' At first, Sunil had wanted to use 'are' rather than 'might be', but his tutor reminded him that he could only test his ideas in one specific setting, where he would not have a 'representative' sample (see Chapter 4). Sunil went into his tutorial thinking that his 'Thomas the Tank Engine' idea might allow him to make a far-reaching finding, but now he begins to contemplate the highly complex nature of research. It certainly was a lot to learn. Never mind, even if it did only work in his classroom, he would still be able to help Arif, Josh, Devon and all his other little guys. Sunil walks past a newsagent, glancing at the headline: 'Confirmed: girls are smarter than boys' in the window. When he realises this relates to the newspaper he usually buys, he selects a different one, after noting their headline: 'Controversial gender research debate'.

Reading strategically and setting the research project in the context of the underpinning literature

This is a skill that can only be fully developed by practice, rather like riding a bike. Your tutor can give you pointers towards the relevant body of literature for the project topic that you have chosen, but they cannot tell you how to make your final selection; you have to do that. You will eventually find that 'practice makes perfect' (or, more honestly, that 'practice makes *better*'!) and if you go on to study at the postgraduate level you will find that one of the results of the process that you are now undertaking is that you will become more adept at working out which book/article to read, and which one is unlikely to be relevant. At all stages of your academic progress you should be able to use a journal article abstract to consider whether it is worth reading further, or whether you should move on to the next article. You may find it helps to record full references for articles that fall into the 'not sure' category, reading the most obviously relevant first and then going back if what you have now read makes you think that an article you rejected earlier might in fact have some level of relevance. As you become more experienced within your topic area, you will find out who the 'key researchers' are in this particular area; once you have got to this stage, you can search for their work using their names (see Chapter 2).

Once you have decided upon your methodology you should also read up on literature that is relevant to this, and a small body of this reading should feature in your literature review. Unless the methodology itself is centrally relevant to your research topic (e.g. studying something in a novel way) this should however not take up a significant amount of your literature review word limit.

The test of a literature review is how skilfully its contents guide your reader towards your research question, which should be presented in the final paragraph. As someone who has marked many research projects, I am very familiar with the feeling of disappointment that arises when I realise that the research question the student is presenting me with has very little to do with the body of literature that has informed the review above! One way to look at your literature review is like a 'funnel', which introduces and debates literature in the areas that are generally relevant to the research question, then extracts particular theories and concepts from these areas to move conceptually into the project's research question.

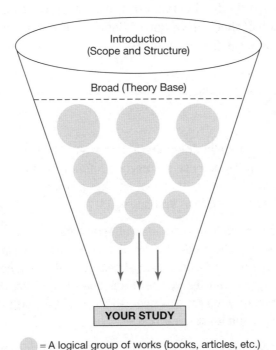

Figure 3.1 The funnel method of structuring a literature review
Source: Hofstee, 2006

Creating a 'thematic' literature review

Literature reviews in academic research conventionally take a 'thematic' approach, where the writer considers specific issues emerging from their research question through examining the literature. Students often find this difficult when they are first starting out, and instead 'list' the relevant literature, hence this has become known as 'the shopping list approach'.

The key issue for the reader is that where the writer takes a thematic approach the literature is presented in a way that is highly relevant to the research in question ('I asked this question of the literature and this is what I found'), while the 'shopping list approach' just lists readings that the writer deems appropriate, but there is no clear guide to the reader as to how and why the author has proposed that these areas of the literature are specifically relevant to the research question(s). In effect, in the thematic approach the writer directs the text; in the 'shopping list approach' the readings quoted take over, and the reader then has to make various guesses as to why the author has used this selection of readings. Early drafts of the undergraduate literature review typically tend towards the 'shopping list' style. You will need to accept that you will write your literature review several times, and that it is strongly advised that researchers produce the final version of their literature review in partnership with the production of their discussion of findings, *after* carrying out the practical research and analysis (see Chapter 8).

Ellie

... reviews her first attempt at her literature review. She has begun this task with the purpose of inserting references into the text, but begins to realise that what she has produced is what her tutor has referred to as a 'shopping list'.

'The first person to introduce the idea of attachment was John Bowlby. He was the student of Anna Freud, who was Sigmund Freud's daughter. Bowlby provided psychological help for children who had suffered separation from their families due to the Second World War. He found that there was a particular problem that seemed to develop . . . (three paragraphs about John Bowlby and Anna Freud)

'In the 1960s researchers began to question Bowlby's focus on children's mothers. Schaffer and Emerson carried out a longitudinal study of children between *birth and three in Glasgow. Many of these children lived in very large families. Schaffer and Emerson found that they were attached not only to their mothers but to their fathers, grandparents and siblings . . .* (three paragraphs about Schaffer and Emerson's research)

'*Barbara Tizard found that attachment could be quite flexible even after the "sensitive period" that John Bowlby had proposed. She carried out a piece of longitudinal research in several stages, considering the attachments of children who had been fostered, and then either returned to their own families or adopted . . .* (two paragraphs about Tizard's research in which Ellie realises that it is obvious that she has struggled to understand the complicated methodologies of the various studies)

'*Jay Belsky carried out several studies on the emotional development of children who attended daycare before they were three years old. These studies had different results, which seemed to depend on the settings in which the children attended. The first study found that*' . . . (two paragraphs about Belsky's studies)

Ellie consults her tutor, who helps her to write the following introductory paragraph for her literature review:

'*This literature review will consider studies of attachment across sixty years of research, starting with John Bowlby who introduced the concept of attachment, based on his work with children who had been separated from their parents in the Second World War. Subsequent researchers have questioned different aspects of his theory, Schaffer and Emerson in terms of the complete focus on the role of the mother, and Tizard in terms of the existence of a discrete 'sensitive period' between the ages of birth and three. The review will then consider modern attachment research, in particular studies carried out with children in daycare, such as those by Jay Belsky.*'

Ellie's tutor also suggests that she avoid using lengthy quotes, instead summarising the points made by the authors in her own words. The tutor explains that this has the double benefit of helping the writer to make the most of the word limit, and to clarify the contents of the literature in the process of creating the summary. Ellie begins to see how she can select the aspects of the theories concerned to inform her research question in the 'funnel' fashion, rather than simply present her assessor with 'everything I know' from the reading that she has done to inform her dissertation.

A clear advantage of the thematic style is that it tends to lead to less irrelevant 'waffle' as the author is guided by the thematic approach to maintain relevance to the research question they are attempting to investigate, which is always

▶

helpful when writing to a word limit. Ellie's tutor gives her one more tip to keep on the thematic 'path': never start a paragraph with an author's name, but with a reference to the theme you intend to address; for example, rather than *'Bowlby proposed that mothers were the most important person in the world to a baby . . . .'* which tempts the writer to fixate on Bowlby's theory, begin with the more discursive: *'Attachment theorists' construction of the role of the mother has changed quite considerably over time . . . .'*

Thinking (and writing) critically

Undergraduate students often find this the hardest skill to learn. Students have said to me in the past: 'How can I question the views of someone who has spent their whole career researching in this area?' The answer is: with the views of another such researcher, many of whom will make their reservations with the original theory quite plain in their work, both in terms of re-testing it, and raising issues relating to the methodology of the previous researcher. Attachment theory, which informs Ellie's review, is an excellent example of this. It began with a basic theory from a mid-twentieth century researcher whose findings relating to the devastating impact of war upon children are still relevant today, but who was found by subsequent researchers in the field to have been heavily influenced by his culture, particularly with respect to very traditional concepts of gender roles in parenting, in terms of the recommendations he made from the basis of his research findings. By reflecting on the literature in this way it is possible for undergraduate students to produce a critical and analytical literature review that is worthy of a very high grade. They will of course go on refining these skills if they continue into postgraduate education!

Florentyna

. . . consults her tutor about the complex nature of 'criticism'. The more she reads in European literature, the more critical she becomes of the practice within her own setting, with its highly prescribed outdoor play arena, filled with

plastic toys and areas that are policed by practitioners frequently informing children about 'correct' and 'safe' ways to play with these. The tutor suggests that Florentyna continue to read literature relating to 'communities of practice' in childcare, attempting to actively relate these to the plethora of guidelines and curricula produced by the English government over the past twenty years to prescribe practice with children under five. After a couple of weeks, Florentyna finds that she is more, not less confused. Now she is less inclined to think of her colleagues as 'ignorant' and this has made her less sure about how she intends to use her 'forest school area' to remedy all the problems that she initially perceived. Her tutor deems this to be a very satisfactory progression.

Reflection point

Developing critical skills usually results in becoming less rather than more sure about what is wrong within a practice setting, and how to go about addressing issues. Keeping in mind the old proverb that 'fools rush in where angels fear to tread', consider what benefits might result from the training of potential leaders in Early Years, and helping them to appreciate that the most effective change may sometimes be best accomplished gradually.

Recording for referencing

When you begin reading for your literature review, you might find the following template useful. It can be used flexibly as a printed sheet, as a series of Word documents, or turned into an Excel spreadsheet or database, whichever you find more suitable for your own purposes. As indicated above, you will revise your literature review constantly throughout your project. One aspect of this process can be suddenly realising (often during or directly following your practical investigation) that an article or chapter you thought was peripheral to your investigation actually has key significance. If you keep meticulous summaries of all the sources you have read, this will take a huge amount of stress out of the 'revisiting' process, and of course also save time, which is the most precious currency within the dissertation/practitioner research module process. As such, keeping record sheets of this nature can make a significant difference to a student's potential grade.

Record of journal article

Name of author(s)
Title of paper:
Date of paper:
Date accessed:
Information necessary to retrieve the paper (e.g. journal details, URL etc.)
Review of literature or report of empirical research
Research questions/purpose of review of the literature
Summary of research/review (one paragraph only – the article abstract should help here)
If empirical research: sample/participants
If empirical research: methodological design
If empirical research, results obtained; if review of literature, overall summary of research discussed
Author's interpretation of research results or of literature reviewed
Your own interpretation of the information within the paper (summary: one or two paragraphs maximum)
Potential for practical applications

Reflection point

Why not design similar sheets for recording your reflections upon books/multi-media sources?

Sectioning the project write-up

By the time you come to the end of your literature review, you should be moving into your practical research. At this point you will find that 'what goes where' in the write-up will become more important to you and, as such, now is a good time to consider creating different files on your PC for each section of the report. While you may have to eventually submit your project electronically in one unitary file, it is a good idea to work with separate documents while the write-up is 'in progress' as this will help to ensure that you put the right information into the right section as you go. It is relatively easy to 'cut and paste' the contents of each document into one unitary document at the end, should this be necessary.

All universities and colleges will have their own advised structure for research reports, but the differences are likely to be slight. This section provides a very typical structure, widely used across the English Higher Education system. As always, if in doubt, consult your tutor. The word 'dissertation' is used in the following section, but practical practitioner research projects will generally use similar write-up conventions.

Abstract

This follows the title page. It gives a carefully summarised description of the topic, methods and main findings of the dissertation. Comprehensiveness and succinctness are the characteristics of a good abstract. Although the abstract is presented first in the dissertation, it is best written in the final days of text construction, when you will have the necessary overall grasp of the project to enable you to present it in such a heavily summarised format. If you are reading this at a point where you feel this will never be the case (usually at the point between finishing the first draft of the literature review and before beginning the practical research), do have faith that it will!

Introduction

This places the dissertation in relation to its general topic and to other work on the subject. It will include the aims and objectives of the dissertation, a summary of its relation to ideas and approaches in the literature, and indicate the framework of the discussion and structure of the dissertation as a whole. Again, this is best written after the later sections of the dissertation have been finalised.

Literature review

This section contains a review of a selection of literature relevant to the area of study. It should:

- Show that the writer has engaged with the key issues that relate to the studied topic

- Demonstrate engagement with relevant academic literature and debates

- Close with a summary of the key issues from the literature reviewed, creating a clear exposition of its relationship to the dissertation topic, leading into a clear outline of the research question(s).

Methodology

This section needs to include a general theoretical explanation of the methods you have used to collect and analyse data. The following issues need to be addressed in the methodology section of your write-up:

- What methods have you chosen?

- Why have you chosen these methods?

- What data will be collected?

- What materials will be used to collect the data?

- How will the data be collected (e.g. places, schedules)?

- Who are the intended participants?

- What measures must be taken to make sure that the research is ethically enacted?

Presenting results/discussion sections

The results and discussion can be presented in the same or in separate sections. In general, qualitative research will be presented in a combined findings and analysis section, and quantitative research in separate results/discussion sections. There are various compromises for research using both qualitative and quantitative methods. A final decision on how to present these section(s) should be made in consultation with your tutor.

Findings/analysis

This structure is usually used in a report that describes the collection and analysis of qualitative data. It combines the results and analysis process in one section. It is most commonly used where semi-structured interview or focused observation data has been gathered and thematically analysed. In a section of this nature, you should explain the process by which you drew themes from your data (see Chapters 4 and 5), then clearly present the themes that you have identified one by one as headings, each one followed by a paragraph of analysis structured in the way that is outlined in the 'Discussion' section below. You should also provide an overall conclusion on general linkages or emergent disparities between your identified themes.

Results

This section reports on data collected, and presents an overall summary of your findings. The data collected should be presented in a clear format and a commentary provided that analyses/interprets the results so that readers can make sense of the findings. This will involve a thorough presentation of the data in a combination of textual explanation, data matrices (tables), diagrams and charts (see Chapter 7). Do not simply present your data and expect your reader to make their own sense of it – this will lose a lot of marks! Lengthy data samples and calculations should be placed in the appendices.

Discussion

This section is the topic of Chapter 8, where it is examined in detail. In summary, it should:

- Explicitly identify the important issues arising from the findings, explaining their significance, with a key emphasis on practice

- Relate the findings to those of other studies/theories you have cited in the literature review, focusing particularly upon unexpected findings and inconsistencies between the findings that you have made and those found by previous researchers

- Comment upon triangulation of data, where different methods used made similar or disparate findings

- At the end of this section, it is useful to undertake a brief reflexive analysis of why you might have framed your research question(s) in the way that you did, and why you might have interpreted your data in this/these particular way(s).

Conclusion/recommendations

This short section should:

- Reflect on your research 'journey', in particular where you feel that things could have gone better, and how you would improve your methodology if you were to undertake further research in this area. You should also offer suggestions for future research that might further your area of investigation.

- Make recommendations for improving practice that can be shown to have logically emerged from your research.

Note that there is no penalty for inconclusive findings as long as you *recognise* these as such.

References

Compile your references as you use the material, rather than trying to undertake referencing as a huge task as you come to the end of your dissertation construction. Noting your references on cards, and putting these in alphabetical order in a box file as you go along can be helpful; also see the example record sheets above.

Don't forget to note page numbers for material you intend to use in 'quote' form. The references must be presented in your text in accordance with the referencing system used by your institution (see Chapter 9).

Appendices

These will contain associated paper materials, for example diary extracts, observation sheets, interview transcripts and calculations. Never rely on an appendix to extend the specified word limit. A reader should not have to refer to an appendix to grasp any major points that you wish to communicate within your text. Appendix materials should be for any extra information that a reader may wish to access if they are interested, e.g. additional information on the content of an interview; an exact replica of the questionnaire that you used.

For further information on each section of the report, consult the relevant chapter in this book. The above is intended as an introductory outline only.

Using the 'passive voice' in academic writing

The use of the 'passive voice' or 'third person' in academic writing is a convention which has descended from the biological sciences into the social sciences and, as such, is the source of ongoing debate. Your institution should have a general advice document for students engaged in academic research, instructing them what is expected in this respect.

My own advice to students has always been to use the 'passive voice' where at all possible; for example, it is very easy to say that 'the questionnaires were distributed' rather than 'I gave out the questionnaires'. However, use of the passive voice can sometimes become difficult in social science research. An example is in reporting participant observation (see Chapter 5), for example 'the child gave all the crayons back to me, and I said "what colours do you want?"' Students may then produce stilted grammatical constructions to comply with the 'passive voice' convention in such cases that hamper the clarity of meaning; for example, 'the child gave the crayons back to the practitioner and the practitioner said . . .' rather muddies the waters as to which practitioner this might be! As always, if in doubt, seek your tutor's advice.

Nick closes his PC, determining that this version of his literature review will take him into his methodology. On the one hand, he feels like he has written it a thousand times, but on the other, he is pleased with the way that it has developed his thinking on the topic. . . .

Ellie has made a start on 'thematicising' her literature review, but realises that the time has come to make a start on her practical research. She reflects that the process of creating the literature review has made her feel less driven by the need for perfection. She now realises that even eminent researchers are not perfect, and, that being the case, there is certainly hope for her little project. . . .

Florentyna decides on completing the first draft of her literature review that, in order to focus on her methodology, she needs to distance herself from her misgivings about the current practice in her setting. If she can create a little 'forest school area' on the site, and bring the children and practitioners into its culture and show them its benefits, then perhaps that will have a wider impact on all the issues she has been concerned about in the practice environment. . . .

Sunil has his literature review written up in discrete topic-based sections at the point his tutor proposes that it is time to move on into the practical research. Sunil has some very useful ideas relating to activities that he can pilot with 'the lads' and is determined to follow his tutor's advice in terms of making small changes and analysing these carefully, rather than making dramatic changes and losing the thread of the analysis. He has arranged an appointment with both the nursery and reception teachers to get the 'go-ahead' for his plans. . . .

Reflection point

You probably feel you know our students quite well by this point. Try to predict what problems they might meet next on their research journey, and make some brief notes on this topic. You can contemplate these predictions as you move through the following chapters.

Chapter 4
Introduction to methodology

Clive Opie and Pam Jarvis

Introduction

The first three chapters of this book have concentrated on the preparation and planning of your research and identifying the importance of undertaking a literature review. These aspects of research are critical and complementary. Planning and preparation help to ensure the best prospect of success, but this should be informed from your literature review which will identify research processes that others have undertaken in your chosen area of research. What this chapter will do is start to look at 'research terminology' such as methodology, approaches and methods (or procedures, as we will call them) which are likely to be most appropriate for the kind of research you will be doing. Whilst it does introduce some other terms, these will be kept to an essential minimum. The main aim of this book is to provide you with a practical guide to research in Early Years settings, and as such this will be the focus of this chapter.

Research terminology

This chapter will not provide an exhaustive discussion of research terminology. If this is required, there are other texts that can be referred to, e.g. Cohen *et al.* (2008); Opie (2004a); and Clough and Nutbrown (2002). It will however explore a few terms to set the scene and provide you with a little insight into the development of educational research, and the methods that undergraduate Early Years and Education students most typically use for their research.

Methodology

This refers to the theory of acquiring knowledge about research methods, or as Sikes (2004: 16) puts it:

> Methodology is concerned with the description and analysis of research methods rather than with the actual, practical use of those methods. Methodological work is, therefore, philosophical, thinking, work.

There is often confusion between the terms methodology and methods, which is why we prefer and use the term procedures to describe the practical aspects of research in this chapter.

The confusion between methodology and methods is widespread and perhaps easier to appreciate is Clough's and Nutbrown (2002: 22) analogy:

> We suggest that, at its simplest, this distinction can be seen in terms of methods [procedures] as being some of the ingredients of research, whilst methodology provides the reasons for using a particular research recipe . . . Thus methodology starts by quite simply asking questions such as: 'Why interview?', 'Why carry out a questionnaire survey?', 'Why interview 25 rather than 500 participants?'

The key point is the need for any researcher to justify and argue their methodological case for choosing a particular research approach and research procedure.

Ontology and epistemology

Before you close this book, read on! These terms may seem really high powered but they are not so difficult to understand and they are important as they form the basis of everything else we will discuss.

Let's start from the premise that there is no 'right' way of undertaking educational research. Rather, the 'right' recipe will depend on the combination of

Sunil

. . . finds that the range of research methods whirl around in his head. He does not feel able to make even the first decision about which ones might be most suitable. His tutor tells him to think about what he wants to achieve with his research activities. 'To help the lads with their reading', he replies. 'OK', says his tutor, 'let's start from that basis, and move on to how you are going to evaluate the activities that you develop when you have at least made a start on designing them!'

Reflection point

Sunil feels better now he has a short-term goal to work towards. Can you begin to set some short-term goals for your own project? If so, you are beginning to learn how to 'eat the elephant' we introduced in Chapter 1!

Based on: http://stayontargetcoach.com/author/Admin/page/4/

circumstances that are probably unique to you and the research that you wish to carry out. What is important is that you are aware of the different possibilities (and the advantages and disadvantages of each) and explain and justify your chosen methodology to those reading your work.

There are some 'better' ways than others and ultimately your methodological stance, the research approach you will use and the particular research procedures you use will depend on your ontological and epistemological views. Ontology and epistemology are two methodological terms.

Ontology: is concerned with assumptions about social reality and whether a person perceives this to be as 'external, independent, given and objectively real, or, instead as socially constructed, subjectively experienced and the result of human thought as expressed through language' (Sikes 2004: 20). As we shall see shortly, how a person views the social world will influence the research procedures they will use, just as Florentyna found that the way people view the world influences the constructions that they create about 'suitable' play activities for children.

Epistemology: concerns the very basis of knowledge, basically on whether:

> it is possible to identify and communicate the nature of knowledge as being hard, real and capable of being transmitted in a tangible form, or whether knowledge is of a softer, more subjective, spiritual or even transcendental kind, based on experience and insight of a unique and essentially personal nature.

> (Burrell and Morgan 1979: 2)

Let's simplify this a little in terms of choice of research procedures. If your assumption is that knowledge is 'real', then it ought to be possible to observe, measure and quantify it. If, on the other hand, knowledge is regarded as more subjective and based on experience then a researcher will have to ask questions of those involved in the research. Keep this distinction in mind while we introduce some other terms and then pull it all together. In order to further your understanding of these terms you might also find the details given by Sikes (2004: 18-24) useful.

Positivism and interpretivism

Oh no, not more philosophical terms! Bear with us, all will become clear. Remember we have just presented epistemology as having two opposing views with respect to the assumptions about the basis of knowledge. We have also said that depending on which you subscribe to will determine your approach to research and define your research procedures.

Positivism: assume you view 'knowledge as being hard, real and capable of being transmitted in a tangible form', then you would use a research approach which mirrors that of the natural sciences, structured observation, experiments, control of variables etc. You would not be particularly interested in

involvement with the participants in the research. This approach to edu
research is regarded as *positivism* and those subscribing to it as *positi*

Interpretivism: this is now easy to understand. Assume you view 'knowledge
as of a softer, more subjective, spiritual or even transcendental kind, based on
experience and insight of a unique and essentially personal nature'. You would
now be deeply interested in the participants in your research, attempting to
understand their feelings, beliefs, reasoning, thoughts, perceptions; ideas
would be of paramount importance to your research, and you would reject the
ways of natural science. This approach to educational research is regarded as
interpretivism and those subscribing to it as *interpretivists*.

Nick

. . . has been contemplating the differences between posi-
tivists and interpretivists. He came across the definition in
his first degree, and quickly dismissed any potential benefits of the interpretivist approach. As he is riding his bike
to work he begins to consider that he is not as much of a
positivist as he used to be. At least, he thinks to himself, in terms of my work
at school and the importance of the relationships and understandings of all the
people involved. I was initially approaching my research in a very positivist way,
thinking that the most important aspect of the situation was the measurable
mathematical competence of the teaching assistants. I guess my first degree
ethos was much more appropriate to positivist views of the world than the way
that teachers have to work with different people, staff, pupils *and* parents. By
this time he has arrived at school to be met with a cheery 'good morning' from
one of his previously sullen TAs. Perhaps there is more to interpretivisim than
the inexact waffle I first thought, he contemplates as he walks down the corridor to his classroom.

Cohen *et al.* (2008) discuss the above terms in a much more detailed (and
readable) way and you will also find texts that use the terms objectivist for
positivist, and subjectivist or anti-positivist in place of interpretivist. You
will also find positivism and interpretivism referred to as research 'paradigms' where a paradigm is used as a collective term for a set of coherent and appropriate research approaches and procedures for the research
being undertaken. Whatever terms are used, the underlying principles are as
detailed here.

Ellie

. . . feels rising panic as she tries to cope with the concepts of ontology, epistemology, positivism and interpretivism. Surely, she had signed up for a degree in Early Childhood Studies, not in philosophy? Her tutor asks her whether she thinks there is a definitive answer to her question about the relevance of attachment to the role of the key person. Ellie thinks for a moment. 'Well, I did when I started, but I am not so sure now', she says, thoughtfully. 'So', says her tutor, 'is it fair to say you started off as a positivist but you are now much more inclined to take the interpretivist approach?' 'Ah', replies Ellie, 'I am beginning to see what you mean.'

Quantitative and qualitative

These terms refer more specifically to the types of research procedures you might use.

Quite simply, **quantitative** refers to procedures concerned with the collection of numerical data or data which can be number crunched – think quantity if it helps. There is no definitive procedure concerned specifically with quantitative research. Whilst experiments and questionnaires (particularly market research) are often linked to the collection of quantitative data, observations (through the use of coding sheets) and interviews can all generate such data.

Qualitative refers to procedures concerned with the collection of data which reflects the 'concern with feelings and perceptions and an admitting of different perspectives' (Burton and Bartlett 2005: 18). Here experiments and questionnaires are far less important – and some would say are an anathema to qualitative research – whereas observations and interviews which set out to explore such 'personal viewpoints' are far more appropriate.

Now let's pull the terminology together and perhaps the easiest way to do this is with a diagram. Figure 4.1 pulls together all the terms above and hopefully you will see how they link. It is not necessarily important to remember all the terms although doing so will undoubtedly help your understanding, but being able to recognise their significance in terms of designing your research is important. Deciding why you would choose one research approach over another and particular research procedures over others is critical, and the quality of your final piece of research will stand or fall on such decisions being correctly taken from the outset – with the help of your tutor.

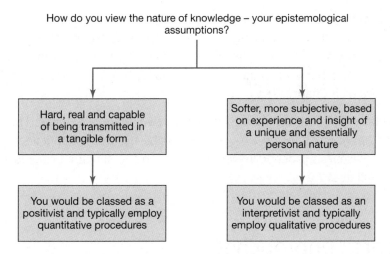

How do you view the nature of knowledge – your epistemological assumptions?

Hard, real and capable of being transmitted in a tangible form

Softer, more subjective, based on experience and insight of a unique and essentially personal nature

You would be classed as a positivist and typically employ quantitative procedures

You would be classed as an interpretivist and typically employ qualitative procedures

Figure 4.1 An overview of research terminology

Figure 4.1 would seem to offer a simple link (some would say too simple) but in essence, in our view, it provides all that is really necessary to grasp the basics of educational research. If anything, it might suggest quantitative and qualitative research are somewhat separate entities, whereas in reality there is often a blurring of these as you will no doubt come to experience. Indeed, undertaking aspects of each is one of the key aspects to what we refer to as *'triangulation'*. Whilst we will not go fully into triangulation here (see Chapter 7 for this), it basically means 'checking one's findings by using several points of reference' (Burton and Bartlett 2005: 28). Involving the use of a range of research procedures, collecting information from a variety of contributors, teachers, pupils

Florentyna

. . . considers triangulating the data in her methodology. She has now cleared the area she is to use for her 'forest school' and begun to involve the children in some ongoing projects, many relating to planting in particular areas. She is nearly ready to conduct some observations with children engaged in free play in the area, and has been asked by her tutor to consider how she will 'triangulate' her findings. She decides to create a questionnaire for her colleagues in order to discover their perspectives on her initiatives. She thinks that this will also help her to situate her little 'forest school' within the culture of the setting, which she now realises will be to the benefit of all concerned.

etc. or collecting data from a variety of sources are examples of triangulation methods, for example observing children's response to an activity and then interviewing the staff about their opinions of it. If your observational data and the opinions of other staff generally correspond, this increases the **reliability** of your data (see Chapter 1).

To complete this chapter we will look into two other elements. The first is Research approaches which we use to describe the overall approach to your work, and Research procedures which refers to the specific procedures your research will use.

Research approaches

There is a wide range of these but for the purposes of your work only two are regarded as really appropriate, the **case study** and **action research**.

The **case study** provides 'an opportunity for one aspect of a problem to be studied in some depth within a limited timescale' (Bell 1999: 10). As Bell goes on to say (1999: 11):

> The great strength of a case study method (approach) is that it allows the researcher to concentrate on a specific instance or situation and to identify the various interactive processes at work.

Again you will find that the texts already identified in this chapter explore the case study approach and cite numerous examples. What is worth considering about the examples is the issue of sample size. As Opie (2004b: 74) note, this is meaningless as it 'could involve a single person, a group of people within a setting, a whole class, a department within a school'.

The essence of **action research** is that it enables a reflective cyclic process to be brought to bear on the understanding of the problem at hand. This is probably most easily understood through the following diagram (Figure 4.2).

This does somewhat simplify the potential complexity of the approach and the criticisms of it in that it starts with the premise that there is a problem rather than developing a broader understanding of the learning process (see Burton and Bartlett 2005: 37-39), but it does encapsulate the main structure. Cohen *et al.* (2008: 297-312) and Opie (2004b: 79-87) also provide further details.

In summary, action research involves identifying an aspect of practice you think you can improve, making a small change, evaluating its effects and

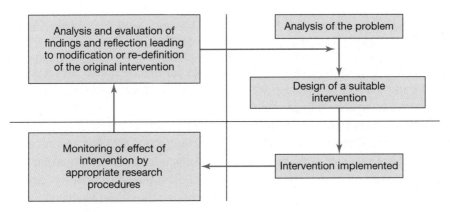

Figure 4.2 A diagrammatic view of action research

then making a further small change and evaluating again, going round the cycle as many times as you deem necessary. Most undergraduate students find that they can only go once or twice around the action research cycle in the time they have to do their practical research, but many are encouraged by their settings to continue the process after the submission of their assignment, if it is having positive effects upon practice. Case study describes a small-scale study in one setting where a topic is closely investigated but nothing is systematically changed during the duration of the investigation.

Sunil

. . . is beginning to realise that action research is more suitable for the project that he has in mind. One of the problems that has emerged from his setting is that, where pre-literacy activities are offered within continuous provision, it is overwhelmingly girls who access them. What he plans to do is to introduce new activities and create an observation schedule (see Chapter 5) that allows him to measure whether this increases the number of boys freely choosing to access the pre-literacy activities. His first idea relates to introducing the concept of 'station names' and 'tickets' into an outdoor activity where the boys are guided to pretend that they are train drivers riding the bikes around a circuit that has been chalked on the tarmac playground. Sunil will ask their help in deciding where the stations should be situated and what they are going to be called, and then ask those who choose to be involved in the activity (boys and girls) to help him to make the tickets for teddy bear 'passengers'. He

▶

finds the nursery teacher to be very interested and helpful, but the reception teacher is rather dismissive.

He discusses this with his tutor, and she points out that he should reflect on the fact that the reception teacher will now be concerned with assessing 'her' children in readiness for filling in individual EYFS profiles, and suggests it might be helpful to find out which formative assessment guidelines the reception teacher used. He could then try to show how his activities encouraged the development of the relevant skills and knowledge. Sunil left the tutorial thinking that sounded like a lot of extra work, and anyway, hadn't the latest review promised to cut back on a lot of the paperwork, remembering the recent headlines in one of the broadsheets? It seemed self-evident to him that his activities would help promote boys' interests in pre-literacy.

Reflection point

Gately and Gately (2001: 40) suggest that the eight components of successful colleague relationships in education are as follows:

1 Interpersonal communication

2 Physical arrangement

3 Familiarity with the curriculum

4 Curriculum goals and modifications

5 Instructional planning

6 Instructional presentation

7 Classroom management

8 Assessment

Consider where Sunil and the reception teacher may not be making sufficient efforts in these respects.

There are other approaches, such as **experiments, grounded theory** and **ethnography**. However, experiments are unsuitable for undergraduate research in Early Years settings as they raise all sorts of ethical issues, and grounded theory requires a systematic rigour that is unlikely to be attainable in the time you have for your research. Full ethnography requires a degree of immersion which will be impractical, but you may be able to use some very basic elements of this approach in observational research; this will be covered in Chapter 5. Those of you really interested in exploring further research approaches will be able to find discussion of them in the texts cited in this chapter.

Research procedures

The final part of this chapter will be devoted to exploring those procedures (methods) or practical tools commonly used in educational research of the type you will be involved in, with regard to questionnaires and interviews. Observational research will be covered in the following chapter.

Questionnaires

Questionnaires are typically used when responses from a relatively large number of people are needed, and where it would be impractical or impossible to get them in other ways, e.g. for each person to be interviewed in person.

Whilst questionnaires may seem easy to devise, nothing could be further from the truth. Although it is, of course, important to prepare a questionnaire thoroughly before you use it, there is a fundamental question to ask yourself before producing a questionnaire, which is: what is my methodological reason for doing so? As Bell notes, questionnaires:

> can provide answers to the questions What? Where? When? and How?, but it is not so easy to find out Why? Causal relationships can rarely if ever be proved by a questionnaire. The main emphasis is on fact-finding.

(Bell 1999: 14)

If we heed this note, and it is wise to do so, then questionnaires lend themselves well to quantitative work but not qualitative work. Some argue if you ask open-ended questions, ones that require a concerted written response, then surely a questionnaire could gather a body of qualitative data. It might, if respondents filled them in, but notoriously they do not as they take longer for participants to complete and the responses you get invariably do not allow you to explore complex issues or experiential nuances – interviews and observations are much better for this.

Assuming a questionnaire is a useful procedure to use in your research, then you need to think very carefully about exactly what information the questionnaire needs to gather, the best method of doing so and, although this is often ignored, how the information collected will be analysed. Does each question have a purpose – if not, why are you asking it? If the age or gender of a respondent is not crucial then why ask participants to give this information; you might be amazed how many student researchers do ask for such information simply as a matter of course! Can you devise questions which are straightforward to read and yet sufficiently probing to yield worthwhile information for your research? When you begin to explore these questions, you can see that a questionnaire (especially a short one, poorly prepared) may not allow you to explore what you wish to explore, and/or to the depth that you require. In the undergraduate Early Years or Education research, project questionnaires are however frequently used as a device for triangulation of findings, for example asking relevant adults (practitioners or parents) for information that adds to data collected via an observational approach.

Layout

- Try to make an overall impression with your layout which encourages the respondent to want to read and answer it.

- Give clear instructions relating to how you want participants to complete your questionnaire, e.g. 'Please tick the appropriate box' or 'Circle your replies'.

- Ensure suitable spacing between questions and suitable space for the participants to clearly indicate their answers.

- Be very careful with the ordering of your questions.

- Thank your respondents for being prepared to take part.

Ordering of questions

You want your respondents to reply, so you need to think carefully about the best way to achieve this. After all, if they don't respond, you will not obtain any data! As a rule of thumb:

> it is better to put demographic questions, i.e. those on age, marital status, occupation etc. [if required] towards the end. This is partly because they are uninteresting and partly, being sensitive, they may be resented. Other sensitive questions [that relate to information that is essential to your topic] on areas such as sexual orientation, health, income, professional status etc. should also not come near the beginning of a questionnaire.

> (Sapsford and Jupp 1996: 105)

Also, think very carefully if you need to know someone's name or contact details. People are usually willing to support your research if they have been appropriately prepared and asked but tend to swiftly lose enthusiasm if this cannot be done anonymously. This is also part of your ethical consideration with regard to the anonymity of participants, and the confidentiality of data collected. If it is critical that you have personal details, for example so you can follow up on any interesting responses, then say so at the end of your questionnaire and ask the participants to submit such details if, and only if, they are prepared to be contacted.

Questionnaire construction

It is better to ask carefully designed and quite detailed questions about a few precisely defined issues than the same number on a very wide range of topics.

(Dyer 1995)

A questionnaire is a useful tool to discover people's opinions on a particular topic, but, as Dyer indicates above, first of all, you must remember a basic rule of research: investigate *what*? You need to have a very well defined research question or questions (see Chapters 1 and 3) before moving on to construct your questionnaire; if you do not, you will have no basis upon which to focus your questions to participants.

Closed and open questions

Having carefully defined your topic, you need to define your questions. If you want to collect **numerical** data, you have to use closed questions. For example, 'What do you think about the new Early Years Foundation Stage (EYFS) proposals?' is an open question, whereas 'Do you think the new EYFS guidelines will be a positive development?' is a closed question. Where you ask closed questions you can devise a scoring system and collect data that can be converted to numerical scores. You can allocate scores for different answers such as 'yes', 'no' or 'not sure', and if you then present the question to different groups (for example, parents and practitioners) you can collect their scores together and compare them.

For instance, you could ask a group of Early Years teachers and a group of teaching assistants: 'Do you think the implementation of the new Early Years Foundation Stage (EYFS) guidelines will be a positive development?' and score their answers 2 for Yes, 1 for Not sure and 0 for No. If one group got a much larger score it would suggest that this set of people (or *demographic group*) might have a particular collective reason for being more positive towards the implementation of the EYFS. Sometimes you may have a prediction (or hypothesis) about what pattern of answers you are likely to get before you start, in this case possibly based on media reports of previous opinion surveys.

Ambiguity and bias

You should avoid very complicated questions or questions that could be interpreted in more than one way. For example, the question 'Do you think the implementation of the new EYFS guidelines is going to create problems for Early Years staff?' is subject to many different interpretations, such as a practitioner being quite positive about how the system is going to work once it is up and running, but very concerned about the transition stage. You should also avoid phrasing questions in an emotive way, for example: 'Do you think the new EYFS guidelines are going to be very difficult to implement?' You should also avoid asking questions in a biased way, such as: 'Do you think the new EYFS guidelines will be one of the best/worst developments in Early Years practice that you can remember?'

The types of questions that can be asked, along with the pitfalls that different question structures can produce, are further discussed in other texts (see Bell 1999, Chapter 8; Opie 2004a, Chapter 6; Burton and Bartlett 2005, Chapter 8 and Cohen *et al.* 2008, Chapter 15). Here we will give you some insight into these pitfalls, and the following examples, with possible solutions, hopefully will help you to realise that designing questions is not as straightforward as you might think.

Imagine that you have designed a questionnaire for parents that contains the following questions:

1 *What type of nursery does your child attend*?

   Without giving some **types** as a list to select from you will invariably have a problem with 'conformity' in answering this question. Parents may also not be knowledgeable enough about different nursery 'types' to answer such a question very accurately.

2 *What criteria were used to employ the care workers in the nursery your child attends*?

   Think about any course you have undertaken and ask yourself if you could answer this question about, say, your tutors? It is an issue of **lack of knowledge** so try to avoid such questions.

3 *Do you think it is a good idea for children under the age of 5 to be taught formal Maths and English?*

One of the problems here is that you are asking two questions in one – a **double-barrelled** question. Break it up into two questions and then you can analyse opinion relating to Maths and then relating to English, which may differ quite considerably. However, it also raises another issue – do people know what you mean by 'formal'?

4 *Do you agree that all working parents should have access to free childcare facilities?*

This is known as a **leading** question inasmuch as it is difficult to answer no to it. This kind of question is probably better explored through an interview.

5 *How much time do you think children under 5 should be allowed to watch television?*

A great deal ☐ A certain amount ☐ Not very much ☐

Here the issue is one of **quantification**. What is a great deal for one person may be just a certain amount for another. The solution is to quantify the time periods, for example 'an hour a day/three hours a day' etc.

Attitude scale construction

One of the most common ways to construct a scoring system for a question-naire designed to collect quantitative data is to use a Likert scale, named after the researcher who invented the method. Instead of asking the question as a question, you turn it into a statement and offer participants either three or five choices of answer. The resulting sentence is referred to not as a 'question', but as an 'item'. For example, *'Overall, I see the implementation of the new EYFS guidelines as a positive development'*. You can then offer participants a choice of three answers (agree, not sure, disagree) or five answers (strongly agree, agree, not sure, disagree, strongly disagree). The five-point scale allows you to measure people's opinions more exactly. You can also reverse the meanings of items so that you can ask similar questions in different formats, so people do not easily guess the purpose of your questionnaire. It is human nature to attempt to make such guesses, and then to give you the answers that they decide that you are likely to expect (social science researchers refer to this occurrence as participants responding to the **demand characteristics** of a particular approach). For example, the item above could be reversed by asking: *'I do not think that the implementation of the new EYFS guidelines will bring many additional benefits to Early Years practice'*.

Your scoring system should then reflect this. For instance, if you are work-ing on the basis that people who are positive about the new EYFS guidelines score highly on your questionnaire, you would score the first question from 5 to 1 on the five-point Likert scale (strongly agree = 5, agree = 4, not sure = 3, disagree = 2, strongly disagree = 1) and the second question from 1 to 5 (strongly agree = 1, agree = 2, not sure = 3, disagree = 4, strongly disagree = 5). You can then produce an overall score for each questionnaire, and compare the combined scores from each group. In this example, it would be possible to measure which group, Early Years teachers or teaching assistants, were more positive about the new EYFS guidelines, or whether there was very little differ-ence. It is also possible to identify the questions where the greatest and least differences between the two groups occurred.

In addition, it is possible to get a *small* amount of qualitative data from a ques-tionnaire by including items that require the participant to finish a sentence. Examples of 'Finish the sentence' items on the topic introduced above could be:

'Overall, I think the effect of introducing the new EYFS guidelines to Early Years practice in England will be. . .'

and

'I think the main effects that the new EYFS guidelines will have on my own prac-tice are. . .'

These can sometimes turn up very interesting answers from participants that reflect deeply held opinions in a way that Likert scale or standard questionnaire answers cannot. For example, one of the authors of this chapter once designed a questionnaire for teenagers who had been diagnosed as 'discouraged' read-ers that included a 'Finish the sentence' item as follows: 'When I think about reading, I feel . . .' which was completed by one participant with 'like killing the man who invented it'!

Sample size and forms of sampling

It is almost certainly not going to be the case within an undergraduate research project in Early Years or Education that you will be using what are known as *inferential statistics,* i.e. where you wish to infer the characteristics of the whole population from which a sample was taken. What is much more likely is that you will be using *descriptive statistics*, i.e. just reporting how many students agreed or disagreed with an item and perhaps splitting your sample further into specific groups such as gender, age or occupation groups. So, to the burning question: 'What should be my sample size?' there is no one correct answer as it will depend on your asking yourself questions such as: 'Is the sample representative of the group I want to look at?' 'Who can I get access to?' Probably the best advice, as with all research, is to discuss such matters carefully with your tutor.

How you formulate your sample throws up other issues. Should it be completely random or hand picked? Should it just be every third person in a group or the whole group? Again there are no right or wrong answers. Suppose you were working across a year group in a school with five classes totalling 150 potential respondents. Do you work with them all? Take one class as representative of the others? Randomly select 15 pupils from each class? Do you need to cater for a gender or ethnic balance? Phew – not straightforward, is it? But here again your tutor will undoubtedly provide some sound advice to help.

Florentyna

... is struggling with the format of her questionnaires. As English is not her first language, she has found it difficult to transform questions into Likert scale 'items', so her tutor has suggested that, as her main method is going to be observation, she stick to asking straightforward questions and 'Finish the sentence' items. Her questionnaire sample is fixed to the small group of practitioners within her setting. She will not make any comparisons between groups, but consider the pattern of responses on a question by question basis. The more she studies her topic, the more sure she becomes that there are many cultural differences between the way that she views 'best practice' and the way that it may be more generally defined within her setting, and this creates many questions in her mind about suitable ways to construct her questions. She emails her tutor to ask for a tutorial focused upon this point.

Reflection point

Why might Florentyna's tutor find it much more helpful to receive her email requesting a tutorial to discuss a specific aspect of her progress than one that came in five minutes before asking 'Can I see you because I have a lot of problems doing my research?'

Pilot study

Ignore this at your peril! You need to pilot or 'test' any research procedure you intend to use. In the case of questionnaires you will be able to check points such as:

- How long did it take to answer?
- Were the instructions clear?
- Were any of the questions unclear or ambiguous? If so, which and why?
- Was there any objection to answering any of the questions?
- Was anything major omitted?
- Was the layout clear and attractive?
- Was the scoring system you devised easy to apply and useful in terms of being able to evaluate the answers you received in the way that you initially envisaged?
- Any other comments?

A final consideration to make is how you intend to distribute your questionnaire and get it returned. If you self-administer it, you can be pretty sure a high response rate is achievable. One very effective way to do this that ensures anonymity is maintained, where you are surveying your colleagues, is to put a questionnaire collection box in the staff room. You will not then know who submitted which questionnaire. Obviously if you do this, and you are comparing answers between two distinct groups, you have to make sure that people are asked to carefully indicate which group they belong to on the questionnaire. If you are not able to self-administer, you could post out questionnaires and provide stamped, self-addressed envelopes for participants. This is a situation to avoid if at all possible, because your costs will rise and your response rate is likely to fall. This, too, is an area to explore during the pilot stage of your research.

Sunil is now pushing time to get started with his research. The scepticism of the reception teacher has not helped him to 'get going' and now he has decided that, if he cuts out the pilot study, he will be back on track.

Reflection point

Imagine you are a classmate of Sunil's and he has confided in you about his intended strategy. Consider what advice you might give him.

Interviews

It has already been noted that the major drawback with questionnaires is that they are not good for answering the question 'Why?' For instance, take:

'Do you think it is a good idea for children under the age of 5 to be taught formal Maths and English?' When asked correctly, responses to this question might tell you that 65 per cent of respondents answered they did not think formal Maths should be taught. Fine, but if we assume that one of the purposes of your research is to ascertain the most appropriate method of delivery of formal Maths, then on the face of it this finding is not particularly encouraging, is it? What you really need to know is 'why' the respondents feel this way. Is it that they don't understand what you mean by 'formal Maths' and if they did they would be far less negative? Getting such information is much better achieved through direct communication and as such we now turn our attention to the procedure of interviewing.

Interview formats

The format can vary from a highly structured and formal interview to a very unstructured and informal conversational approach. Depending on which is used focuses the research paradigm, and the analysis, as the diagram (Figure 4.3) shows; see also Opie (2004c: 119).

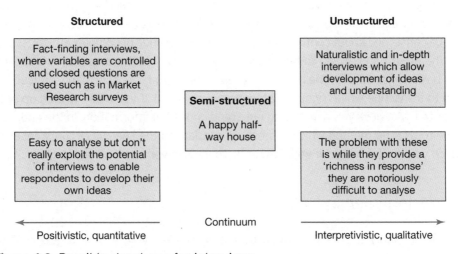

Figure 4.3 Possible structures for interviews

Preparing for an interview

The apparent simplicity of the interview format shown above can, however, be mis-leading. It is important to prepare thoroughly for interviewing. Things to consider include who to interview, how long the interview will last, and where the interview is to take place. Consider the situation, for example, where you are a practitioner in an educational setting and you wish to interview the head teacher or principal of your workplace. Will you interview them in their office, or in 'your' room, or in a neutral setting? How will you arrange the seating? Are you likely to be disturbed? Will you have to try to fit your interview into the demands of a crowded day and perhaps be rushed, or try to do it before or after the normal working day? Will you feel confi-dent in asking 'awkward' questions, and will the head teacher or principal be able to answer such questions honestly? Do you have the interpersonal skills to undertake an interview? – and not everyone has. As Oppenheim (1992: 70) notes:

> The interviewer should be able to maintain control of the interview, to probe gently but incisively and to present a measure of authority and an assurance of confidentiality. Tone of voice, a pleasant and polite man-ner, deportment, choice of dress, the management of personal space, an acceptant and non-judgemental attitude and a willingness to listen should be among the interpersonal skills.

Collecting interview data

Consider how you can effectively record the answers in an interview. Recording the answers might seem the obvious thing to do but, even if technically successful, this can mean many hours have to be spent in listening and transcribing the recordings. Some interviewees will be uncomfortable about the use of a voice recorder as they will be concerned about confidentiality; this creates a range of complex ethical issues. On the other hand, trying to interview and write down answers as they are spoken can be disconcerting for the interviewee, and, unless you take shorthand, difficult for you to transcribe while trying to listen in enough detail. If you delay writing up until after the interview, you risk leaving out some important information. In the end, you have to use the method which is most appropriate to the specific circumstances in which you are carrying out your research; there is never a perfect situation.

Analysing interview data

This is probably the most difficult part as you are trying to pull together sub-jective comments. In general, undergraduate research students are unlikely to interview more than four or five people, and are likely to use a semi-structured approach. What you will need to do is set aside time for transcription of recorded interviews, say 1–2 hours for every 30 minutes of interview data (depending on your typing speed), and then time to 'tease out' the main themes. There is text analysis software available to help but, to be honest, for the amount of data you will have, 'manual' methods to identify **themes** across the range of interviews, such as those described in more detail in Chapter 5, with respect to identifying themes across a range of detailed observation notes, are likely to suffice.

For example, if we look at Florentyna's project, we might predict that 'health and safety' might figure highly if she had chosen to carry out semi-structured interviews with the staff in her setting. If we consider Nick's project, we could posit that if he interviewed his teaching assistants about the ways they construct the concept of 'mathematics' that 'misunderstanding and fear' themes might emerge (if, of course, they agreed to participate and gave completely honest answers!).

You should also consider opinions that are completely opposed to the general direction within the set, and consider why this might be the case. If you choose to feature this in your write-up, you must of course be very careful to protect that participant's anonymity. What is of value is that you aim to use verbatim quotes where you can in the writing of any discussion as these tend to add 'weight' to any arguments you want to make. For this reason, write-ups principally based upon thematic analysis of interviews tend to be best organised around a structure that combines the analysis of data and discussion (see Chapter 8).

If you carry out very brief interviews, you may find analysing their basic **content** to be more appropriate. This involves identifying particular key words or key phrases in each interview, and presenting a chart with the number of times

Nick has decided that he will triangulate his observations of children engaged in his mathematics activities by carrying out structured interviews with his TAs, not only to discover how they view his activities, but also to explore how they felt about mathematics when they were at school. He is also contemplating sending questionnaires to parents to explore the same topic.

Reflection point

What advice would you give to Nick about constructing these interviews and questionnaires, taking into account ethical considerations and the requirement for the participants to feel at ease, in particular both prior to and during an interview?

each word/phrase was mentioned. Do however be aware that content analysis (like most quantitative analyses) produces very 'shallow' data and is in general no better than data gathered by questionnaire at answering the question 'Why?' In general, if you have made the effort to carry out a one-to-one interview it is better to carry out a thematic analysis of the resulting data.

The Mosaic approach

The Mosaic approach was developed by Alison Clark specifically for research in Early Years settings. It focuses upon the *active* participation of young children in research that is focused upon their care and education, and seeks out ways that their opinions can be fully elicited, in the absence of complex language skills. Clark (2004) describes how she carried out very short 'conferences' with children, provided them with cameras to take pictures of things in the setting that they deemed 'important', and asked them to take her on tours of the setting explaining where they were taking her and why. Another related method compatible with the mosaic approach is to ask children to draw a picture of something, for example, an area of the nursery, that might be used for the basis of a semi-structured interview with an older participant, and then ask the child to explain their picture to you, offering a few well selected 'why' and 'so then . . .' follow-up questions, without expecting overly long concentration from the child. An important, related point is that it is possible to get quite insightful comments from children about their activities if carefully considered questions are asked about these directly the child has finished and is moving on to the next thing. Note that 'finished' needs to be sensitively defined. It is bordering upon unethical practice to interrupt a child who is deeply involved in play activity for the sole purpose of your research. If these questions are asked after the child has started on another activity however, the immature memories of children under 7 years do not usually permit them to comment so usefully.

Florentyna reads about the Mosaic approach and decides that she will use it to obtain the children's opinions on the activities that they are undertaking within her 'forest school' area. Her tutor asks her whether she feels she can fully encompass three research methodologies (observation, mosaic and questionnaire) within the word limit for her practitioner research assignment.

Reflection point

If you were Florentyna, how would you answer this question?

Conclusion

This chapter has provided a general introduction to research methodology, and to some approaches that are commonly utilised in Early Years. It is the first of three chapters in this book that are dedicated to methods and approaches. Chapter 5 focuses specifically on the observational approach, recognising that it is the most commonly utilised in Early Years research. Chapter 6 will be wholly dedicated to following our four students through the operation of their individual progress through their practical research activities, considering the problems that they meet and the solutions that they find.

References

Bell, J. (1999) *Doing Your Research Project: a guide for first time researchers in education, health and social science*, Milton Keynes: The Open University.

Burrell, G. and Morgan, G. (1979) *Sociological Paradigms and Organizational Analysis: Elements of the Sociology of Corporate Life*, London: Heinemann.

Burton, D. and Bartlett, S. (2005) *Practitioner Research for Teachers*, London: Sage.

Clark, A. (2004) The Mosaic Approach and Research with Young Children. In V. Lewis, M. Kellett, C. Robinson, S. Fraser and S. Ding (eds), *The Reality of Research with Children and Young People*, 142-56, London: Sage.

Clough, P. and Nutbrown, C. (2002) *A Student's Guide to Methodology: Justifying Enquiry*, London: Sage.

Cohen. L., Manion, L. and Morrison, K. (2008) *Research Methods in Education*, London: Routledge.

Dyer, C. (1995) *Beginning research in psychology: A practical guide to research methods and statistics*, Oxford: Blackwell.

Gately, S. and Gately, F. (2001) Understanding Co-Teaching Components, *Teaching Exceptional Children*, 33(4): 40-47.

Opie, C. (ed.) (2004a) *Doing Educational Research*, London: Sage.

Opie, C. (2004b) Research Approaches. In C. Opie (ed.) *Doing Educational Research*, 73-94, London: Sage.

Opie, C. (2004c) Research Procedures. In C. Opie (ed.) *Doing Educational Research*, 95-129, London: Sage.

Oppenheim, A. (1992) *Questionnaire Design, Interviewing and Attitude Measurement*, London: Pinter.

Sapsford, R. and Jupp, V. (1996) *Data Collection and Analysis*, London: Sage.

Sikes, P. (2004) Methodology, Procedures and Ethical Concerns. In C. Opie, *Doing Educational Research*, 15-33, London: Sage.

Chapter 5
Observation-based research in the Early Years

Jane George, Pam Jarvis and Clive Opie

Introduction

Those of you who are experienced Early Years practitioners will almost certainly have had some experience of observing babies and young children in Early Years care and education settings; indeed some of you may have vivid memories of carrying out what seemed like hundreds of observations to complete your 'Level 3' qualification. Those in initial teacher training are likely to be entering this arena with less prior knowledge, but you will all have been introduced to observations and recording methods that contribute to a child's profile or learning journey. Some of you may also have carried out observations which have helped to inform or review an Individual Learning Plan (IEP) for a child with additional needs. Whilst the skills of watching and recording objectively and drawing conclusions from what you have seen may be second nature to some of you, do note that in this chapter we will re-examine observation as a key component of your *research methodology* toolkit, rather than simply for assessment of an individual child.

When their supervising tutors introduced the idea of observation as a way of collecting data. . . .

Ellie's heart sank! She had invested much time and effort into mastering a range of classical observation techniques, but this was almost 20 years ago and now some of the methods she had used were just vague memories in the back of her mind. As a working practitioner she concentrates on a limited number of observation methods, often imposed by the setting management, some of which she feels are shallow in the extreme, a particular example being the very brief 'post it' note observation that is used to provide basic information for the child's profile. As a deputy manager she now spends significant amounts of time in the office and feels that she doesn't use her observation skills very often, and consequently may not be 'up to speed'.

Nick on the other hand feels comfortable with the idea of observation. He felt confident in using the observation methods chosen by his employment supervisor, and he had learned and practised observation skills during his first degree research module.

Florentyna is currently in the middle of reading about the particular types of activities that form the 'multi-method method', Mosaic. She wonders what might qualify as an 'observation' within this, and writes a note in her journal to ask her tutor.

Reflection point

You will find it helpful at this point in the chapter to jot down some notes about the observation methods you currently use and what you use them for. You could also make a list of observation methods that you have heard of or used in the past. Remember that some of the terminology used may have changed over time.

Introduction to research observation methods

Observation can seem to be a very 'natural' or 'neutral' way of gathering information about a situation. However, it is unlikely to be as natural or neutral as it might appear. One reason for this is that the observer, by their very presence, is likely to change the situation in some way, even if this change can be hard to identify. Thus, for example, if you as the researcher 'sit in' and observe a fellow practitioner's work, how sure can you be that you have not altered the very situation you were trying to observe? Suppose you decide to observe 'friendship patterns' by observing children playing: can you be sure you are observing all the children in a particular friendship group? For example, what if one is 'off sick' that day? Are you able to record interactions accurately? Is your presence as an observer actively changing the situation in some way?

Participant and non-participant observer

There are basically two pathways for you to act as an observer. As a participant observer, you are involved in the process, e.g. practising in a setting while you are also undertaking an observation. It is not difficult to see how this can raise issues, particularly with respect to objective reporting of data and in ensuring you have been able to catch all that you are aiming to observe. As a non-participant observer, the latter problem goes away to some extent, but how, especially with young children and ones you may have helped in the past, do you resist helping them if they ask for it? If you don't help, and you usually do, what will this do to the classroom dynamics – your observations? Also, can you be truly objective about the ongoing events in your workplace? So, how you act out your observational role has implications for your research.

Potential advantages for observational research

Information about the physical environment and about human behaviour can be recorded directly by the researcher. The problems of artificiality created by the experiment are not present in observation; nor are the issues of people giving accurate responses in interviews and surveys either by accident or intention (see Chapter 4).

The observer can make a concerted attempt to 'see the familiar as strange'; this involves writing what researchers term 'thick description', for example describing the area in which you observe the children in painstaking detail and trying to note every single action and utterance as accurately as possible. Many professional researchers use video and analyse the behaviour and language of the participants by stopping and starting the tape every few seconds. It may however not be possible, for both ethical and practical reasons, to carry out a student research project in this very intricate and time-consuming fashion; therefore it is much more likely you will rely on writing detailed observation notes, or dictating such notes into a recording device for later transcription.

Some brief tips for using technology

- The basic requirements for observing are pen and paper.

- Pre-prepared forms are really helpful, especially grids for event and time sampling observations (see the 'target child' method outlined later in this section) and layout plans of your setting for tracking style observations.

- Having a plan for abbreviation such as those used in target child coding makes the recording easier, as does having a plan for 'naming' the participants.

- If you are struggling to record complex verbal interactions you may decide to use a voice recorder. You will need specific consent to do this. At a later time you will need to transcribe the recording to a written record. Some voice recorders will download a file of the spoken record to a computer and some more sophisticated recorders will translate to a Word file but the spoken word is then subject to the vagaries of 'voice-recognition software'!

- If you record using video you build on the benefits from voice recording and you can add body language to the body of information you have gathered and have to deal with. You do however have to consider the impact of introducing a video camera and the ethical implications of this practice.

The slipperiness of 'objectivity'

Being objective is key to all observation, no matter what the purpose, or you stand to lose the advantages of the method outlined above. Record only what you see and hear and do this as accurately as possible. Interpretation, evaluation and links to theoretical concepts and research are aspects to bring into play when you analyse and use the information you have generated. Observation is a key method for studying small children, who cannot 'speak for themselves' in an interview or survey. This does however put an extra burden on the researcher to ensure that they report what has been observed as accurately and objectively as possible, in order to respect the child's point of view as closely as possible.

Sunil

. . . emailed some of his observation notes to his tutor. When he arrived for his next tutorial, he saw she was sitting with a print-out of these, with some phrases highlighted. She passed him the pages, and as he flicked through he saw that, on the first page, she had highlighted: *'Joe and Lennon were having fun'* and *'Josh really enjoyed riding around on the bike'*. . . He looked at her quizzically. 'How do you know that the children were "having fun" or "really enjoyed" something?', she asked. Sunil thought for a moment . . . was this a trick question? She didn't look as though it was, so he responded, 'Well, I guess because they are smiling and laughing and calling out to one another. . . .' 'What you have just said should be the content of your observation', she replied, 'but what you have actually produced here is a subjective opinion in an observation script.'

Sunil's tutor went on to describe an observation that she had carried out when she was in Early Years practice: a child walked across a playground apparently frowning at another child he was known to dislike. She thought for a moment that he was really angry, but then she realised that he had bright sunlight in his eyes, which had created an expression that did not match his emotions. 'What you write in an observation script should always be *what you see*, not *how you are interpreting* what you see. When you get to the evaluation of the observation, that is when you begin to interpret the data. By that stage, you will have a much larger body of information from which to do so.'

'So', said Sunil, 'what you mean is, with respect to the little boy frowning, he moved into the shade and his expression changed, but if he had made a beeline for the child he disliked and started shouting at him, only with that knowledge would you have been able to link annoyance to the expression?' 'That is exactly it', replied his tutor. 'What you are doing in an observation is collecting "real time" evidence. If you put strong interpretations on what you are seeing "on the spot", what you get in your observation script is highly subjective. But if you focus on recording just what you see, you will be able to put meaning into it in a far more objective fashion, only starting to do this once the observation is complete. You should also find that you gather more objective information if you consciously try not to make assumptions about the meanings of people's behaviour. In general, once you start recording in this way, you very quickly stop looking for all the evidence, because you have already started on the interpretation and conclusion.'

'A bit like being a detective', said Sunil. 'Yes', his tutor replied. They both laughed. The tutor continued, 'Research with young children is very much like an exercise in detection – they are only just learning to communicate the contents of their thoughts, which means they are potentially much more difficult to "read" than adults and, of course, even adults can be very difficult.'

'Like the reception teacher at school', reflected Sunil. 'Nothing I do seems to please her.' 'Wait until your activities have some positive results, Sunil', his tutor advised, 'then it might be a very different situation for you.'

Reflection point

Go through some observation notes you have previously produced (not necessarily for your current research) and highlight sections where you have made assumptions, in the same manner as Sunil's tutor. Then carry out at least one practice observation where you consciously attempt to record only objective data. It is a good idea to get into the habit of checking *all* your observation scripts for subjective opinions, not only those you undertake for research. You could very usefully include attempts to improve your ability to carry out objective observations as part of your ongoing CPD.

Observation methods in Early Years and Education

There is a plethora of ways of recording observations from a very simple tick box to more sophisticated category systems (see below). If simply ticking the number of times one child plays in a certain area is enough for your purposes, then fine. If on the other hand you want to know how many different children play in this area and their gender, your observation sheet needs to be a little more detailed. If you want to somehow record not only the latter but 'how' a child plays in the area then you are almost certainly going to need something more comprehensive, for example the Leuven Involvement Scales (see below).

There are a number of texts available which provide excellent support for students learning about observation in Early Years education and care settings. Well-used texts on our bookshelves include:

- Hobart and Frankel, first published in 1994, but still a sound, basic guide

- Riddall-Leech (2008), which looks at observation techniques but also extends into evaluation and links to theory, norms and key documents

- DfES (2005) Standards Unit resources for Health and Social Care, which were produced for Further Education tutors and, when accessed online, include video clips so you can practise your skills

- Palaiologou (2008), part of the 'Achieving Early Years Professional Status' series of books aimed at developing higher level skills, for those with their sights on the postgraduate level.

Types of observation

The main types of observation used in Early Years education and care research break down as follows:

- **Focal or target child observation:** where the observer focuses upon the activity/interactions of a particular child over a specified period of time (unlikely to be longer than 20 minutes as concentration begins to be lost). 'Focal' child observations tend to collect principally qualitative data, and 'target' child observations tend to collect principally quantitative data, but you will find the terms used rather interchangeably across the range of relevant literature. This is a very popular method in Early Years research.

- **Focal or target area observation:** where the observer focuses upon the activity/interactions within a particular area of the setting over a speci-fied period of time (unlikely to be longer than 20 minutes as concentration begins to be lost).

- **'Tracking' observation:** where the observer 'tracks' a child in their activity in free flow play, recording how long they spent in a particular area of the setting, and what they did. It is usual to carry out tracking observations on a series of children. This method of observation is very useful with respect to indicating 'pattern' differences in children's play activities (e.g. girls/boys or older/younger children). This type of observation is also quite useful if you decide to collect data for sociogram analysis (who a child spoke to/interacted with during the period of observation).

- **Time/event sampling:** where the observer records what a particular child is doing, or what is happening in a particular area of the setting at specified time intervals (e.g. either every two minutes, or every five minutes etc.).

Once you have piloted your skills by carrying out some practice observations in your setting to 'trouble-shoot' likely methods, you need to start thinking about how observational evidence can contribute to your research project.

Riddall-Leech (2008: 32) summarises observation methods under four main headings.

Written/narrative	Structured/unstructured/spontaneous/child study/diary/snapshot
Checklists	Charts/profiles/portage records
Diagrammatic	Pie/bar/sociograms/flowcharts
Sampling	Target child/time sample/event sample

If you are trying to select techniques appropriate for your project, you might like to consider whether you are looking for an overview or for detail, what types of questions you are seeking to answer.

Overview

Time sample	Who/where/when/what questions may be answered
Event sample	Looks at an event in context*
Sociograms	Who/when questions may be answered
Tracking	Who/where/when questions may be answered

*Often using the ABC technique (antecedent, behaviour, consequence) in research that relates to behaviour management

Detail

Narrative	Detailed written description of a short period of time
Target child	Summarised and coded observation
Checklist	Comparison of skills shown with norms
Longitudinal	Detailed study over time

Nick

. . . decides that he wishes to carry out observations that generate quantitative data. This will repeat the types of observations he carried out in his first degree (for example, recording in which direction people turn when they enter a shop); as such, he feels this will help him to complete his analysis with the least amount of difficulty. However, when he informs his tutor of this, she immediately questions whether that approach would meet his own criteria of 'interesting and flexible'. Nick contemplates this for a moment, and then sighs, 'You mean that I won't be able to consider how the children actually feel about the activities and why they do or don't get engaged in them.' 'Yes', replies his tutor, 'that is the basic point. You could, for example, collect target area statistics to see how many children access your activities, what gender they are, and how long they stay there. But will that tell you everything you need to know?' Nick admits that would be unlikely. His tutor sends him off with a booklet relating to the 'Leuven' method (see below), which she describes as 'sort of qualitative, but with a quantitative analysis', which Nick finds both intriguing, and a little disturbing with respect to reliability and validity. He realises that this is however a much milder reaction than he would have had at the beginning of the module!

Reflection point

Most student researchers in Early Years settings tend to use a mixture of methods, partly due to the requirement for triangulation, but also because in the end, like Nick, they realise that this will give them the most in-depth understanding of their topic that they can hope for, given the limitations of small sample and short-term research processes. This frequently means that they go on to do some qualitative and some quantitative analysis. At the methodology selection stage, it is very common to feel as if you are going round in circles. The best general advice we can give is that there is no perfect method (or combination of methods), and that you will gain your marks in this respect for having carefully considered the methods available, followed by making a logically considered choice. Part of this consideration should be done in conversation with your tutor and with your module colleagues; the most common mistake for students to make here is to vacillate for a considerable time without discussing the options with anyone, followed by independently making quick-fire choices when they can vacillate no longer. Your tutor will be used to helping dissertation students to make methodological decisions, so do not be worried about approaching them on this point.

Essential considerations

Whatever observation method you think may be suitable for your investigation there are a number of essential points to consider before you begin. Observation raises a specific set of ethical issues that need to be consciously considered and planned for before you begin your research in earnest.

Make no mistake about it, *you* are responsible for the ethical conduct of your research project, not your tutor, or your college. Unethical conduct is unacceptable to all parties – vulnerable children and their families, colleagues, supervisors and managers, heads of settings and tutors. Module tutors are members of professional organisations such as the British Educational Research Association, The Higher Education Academy, and the British Psychological Society. In order to uphold their professional registration they may (rightly) refuse to mark an unethical research project. Hopefully you will heed their advice during the planning stage and avoid these issues.

Being ethical in observational study

Because observation is used so frequently in the day-to-day practice of Early Years settings, this method is more likely to be overlooked by the ethics section of the dissertation than any other research method.

Informed consent from the setting is required before starting any active observation, and is usually given in writing in response to a written request to the head of setting. Occasionally students tell us that this is not necessary as the setting routinely observes children, but what must be recognised is that the setting observes children to inform assessment, profiles and planning, and you are intending to observe to inform your own research project. This is a completely different purpose which will see information being used in a new way, for a new audience outside the setting, and therefore requires specific consent. Any standing consent for observation of children in the setting is not sufficient as it does not recognise how your observations will be used.

You will also need informed consent from the adults in the setting whose co-operation is vital to the success of your project. Your supervisors, colleagues and peers will be affected by your research activity and may even be observed as part of your research. Your observations may highlight excellent practice but could also highlight weaknesses in practice which they may decide to reflect on or they may choose to reject, deny or defend. However they react to your observation, it may impact on your relationship with them; they may lose confidence in themselves or may lose trust in you. If they have agreed to take part in your project, it is essential that they understand that they will be encouraged to review your findings and that your findings may lead to a constructive critical process that informs changes in practice across the setting, and may also lead to constructive suggestions for training needs.

You will require informed consent from the parents and carers of the children you are observing. Whilst they know that their children are observed regularly as part of assessments, profile building and to inform planning, they do need to understand and agree to your observing their children for the purposes of your own research. You must receive their consent to the information you gather being used in a written report which will be viewed by your tutors, and they will only do this if they are confident that you will handle information sensitively and confidentially.

It is also essential to obtain consent from the children who (where possible) should agree to being watched, and, to a developmentally appropriate level, be guided to understand as much as possible about what you are doing, why you are doing it and how the information you gather from them will be used. Clearly this point has to be considered carefully and discussed with your supervisor; sometimes carefully phrased information is required to prevent atypical behaviour every time the children see you with a clipboard, also known as 'the Oscar winning performance'!

Florentyna

. . . is now nearly ready to move into her observations. She has her permissions from her setting and from the children's parents, but she has not yet spoken to the children. She introduces the idea to them at the end of storytime one day, by reminding them that she is not in on Wednesdays because she goes to a type of grown-ups' school (called college) where she is learning about how to teach them. She tells them she has a favour to ask – would they mind her watching them play in the new 'forest area' and writing down what she sees to discuss with her teacher? 'Will your teacher see us?' asked Danny. 'Maybe once when he visits', said Florentyna. 'Can we speak to him?' asked Grace. 'Yes of course', replied Florentyna, 'and do tell him what you think about the forest, too. When I have finished writing down what I see you doing, I am going to write it in a little book, and then I have to give it to him so he can read it.' 'Wow', said Jack, 'we're going to be in a book'. 'Like Harry Potter', said Marie, whose brother was currently immersed in *The Philosopher's Stone*. 'Well, not quite', laughed Florentyna, 'only my teacher and one or two of the other teachers at college will read it.' 'Oh', said Liliya, a little red-haired girl who usually monopolised the biggest crown in the dressing-up area, 'can't we be on TV as well, like Harry Potter?' 'No, DVD, silly', said India, 'or at the cinema', said Anton. 'Not this time, Liliya', said Florentyna, 'but I promise to give a copy of my little book to the centre so your mummies and daddies and all the teachers here can read it, and it can stay here, so you can read it when you are a bit older, if you want.' 'Why do you want to write about us playing?', asked Aidan, a quiet, thoughtful little boy. Florentyna thought for a moment and replied, 'Because grown-ups can't properly remember how they thought and felt when they played when they were little like you, so when we are learning to be teachers we have to learn this from you.' This caused some interested mumbling among the children, on the topic of not realising that grown-ups could *ever* learn anything from children.

'Yes, I want to be in your book', said Liliya, graciously, followed by a chorus of 'and me'/'don't forget to watch me miss'/'I do too'.

Reflection point

Although the names and places have been changed to ensure anonymity, the above example recounts almost exactly what happened when one of the authors of this chapter requested observation permissions from children aged from four-and-a-half to five-and-a-half. The first impression one has as a researcher is how interested and willing to be helpful children are, but beware not to unwittingly exploit this generosity. The author in question determined at this point never to video children's play activities but to carry out focal child observations, dictating 'thick description' observation notes into a mobile recording device for subsequent transcription. Always remember that you are a 'guest' in children's play activity, and that what they may not mind putting to video at five-and-a-half, they may cringe at when they are ten or fifteen. Of course, the answer to this is to destroy the tape when the research report has been graded, but many people forget to do this, and others may even see fit to use such material in training videos without ever requesting any further permission from the child! The 'spoken notes' method, by contrast, allows child participants to maintain their personal privacy while the researcher is able to collect a range of rich data.

David *et al.* (2001) conclude: '*A straightforward notion of children and young people's right or freedom to choose to participate in social research on the basis of the provision of adequate and appropriate information in the school setting especially seems naive. On reflection, our understandings of research with children and young people, and as conducted in the school context, were altogether too simplistic at the outset. Their responses to our topics and methodologies, however, forced reappraisal such that we are now able to see the complex relationships between, and contradictory natures of, notions of children and young people's competence and age, and information and education. We are left with difficult questions about whether consent should, or can, be "informed" or "educated".*'

You may find this article interesting, provoking further reading on this topic.

Being confidential

Finally, on the ethics front, all records should be confidential; should you acciden-tally leave your whole research project (and/or laptop/memory stick) on the bus, it should not be possible for a stranger to identify the setting, the adults or the children from your notes. Also, if you are working on your project in an IT work-shop at your study centre, take great care not to save your work to shared spaces or to leave your work unattended for any period. Participants in your study should be informed that you will take care with their data by using locked storage for paper records and password protection for e-records. That said, always make sure you have back-up copies; dissertations lost in cyberspace at the eleventh hour are not unheard of and tend to create a great deal of heartache for their authors! One reasonably fool-proof way to do this is email a set of up-to-date notes to yourself every time you finish a study session into an email account that only you are able to access with a private log-in. This is far more secure than saving to a multitude of memory sticks, which are even easier to lose on the bus than a laptop, and you will also not find yourself in the position into which one of our students unwit-tingly fell, having been burgled and finding next morning that both her laptop and handbag (in which she kept all her memory sticks) were nowhere to be found!

Observation analysis methods: some examples

Observations can be analysed in a multitude of ways. Some will tend to suggest them-selves (for example the quantitative analyses that are quite obviously associated with tracking and time-sampling). Where an in-depth focal/target child observation has been carried out, taking detailed notes, a thematic analysis that is also most com-monly used for adult interview data can be employed (see below), considering the themes that the child brought into their play activities and/or linguistic interactions.

With regard to versatile observation analyses, one of the earliest methods introduced into the Early Years arena was that of the 'target child' (Sylva *et al.* 1986). The grid used is as follows:

Child's Initials	Gender	Age (Years: Months)	Date	Time
Activity Record		Language Record	Task	Social
1				
2				
3				
4				

(add as many rows as you need)

The authors advise (for the period in which you carry out the observation): 'Write down what the child does in each minute in the activity column. For instance, *"pulls small lump off large piece of dough"* . . . also jot a note down about the activity and materials and whether other children or adults are present. For example, *"table with 2 large lumps of blue dough, 2 other children, helper sitting there"*. Write down what the child says and what other adults say to him in the language column.' (Sylva *et al*. 1986: 234). The authors also suggest a range of abbreviations: 'TC' for target child, 'C' for other child and 'A' for the adult present. You can also use an arrow to show who speaks to whom, for example 'TC→A' means 'target child says to adult'. You can add numbers for subsequent adults and children involved, e.g. C2, A2 and so on.

You code the interaction in the social box, using a range of codes, for example 'SOL' for solitary, 'PAIR' for two people together, 'SG' for small group and 'LG' for large group. Sylva *et al*. suggest a range of codes for the task box including 'SSC' (small scale construction), 'PS' (problem solving), 'PRE' (pretend) and 'WA' (watching). You can find the full range in Sylva *et al*. (1986: 240–43), but you may find it useful to construct your own with reference to the current set of Early Years guidelines in use within your setting. 'Target child' is a very versatile method, which allows you to make both quantitative and qualitative analyses (e.g. *'TC spoke to A ten times, but only once to C who was also engaged in the same activity'* or *'TC watched the other children very closely'*).

Since the introduction of the type of quantitative judgements made by inspection bodies such as OfSTED, a number of complex, broadly qualitative methods have been introduced that have nevertheless been attached to quantitative analysis schedules; these are now quite frequently used for routine observation in Early Years settings. We briefly describe a small range of these below, selected on the basis of their potential usefulness for the purposes of student practitioner research. Student researchers should however always remember that essentially qualitative analyses are being turned into quantitative scales in these specific methods. This raises a number of important questions relating to their reliability and validity which should therefore be raised and discussed in the discussion section of the dissertation.

The Leuven Child Involvement Scale for Young Children

Pascal and Bertram (1977) used this as the observation method in their Effective Early Learning Study (EELS). It was initially developed by Laevers (1994). A summarised description of the method is outlined below.

The child involvement scale consists of two components:

1   A list of 'involvement signals'

2   The levels of involvement in a five-point scale.

The child involvement signals

- **Concentration:** the level of attention the child directs towards the activity

- **Energy:** the effort the child invests in the activity

- **Complexity and creativity:** the level of competence the child shows in the activity, as measured against their previous best efforts; the consideration of whether the child is moving into their 'zone of proximal development' in engagement with this activity

- **Facial expression and posture:** the intensity of the child's posture and facial expression. Do they appear to be completely absorbed in the activity?

- **Persistence:** the duration of concentration that the child gives to the activity, and the ease/difficulty of distraction

- **Precision:** the attention to detail within the activity

- **Reaction time:** how quickly a child reacts to further stimuli within the activity, showing motivation and keenness

- **Language:** how a child talks about a particular activity, e.g. do they ask to do it again, or state that they enjoyed it?

- **Satisfaction:** how proud a child is of their achievements within the activity (N.B. This does not have to relate to satisfaction with a specific product – it could be satisfaction with an experience.)

Child involvement scale

The child involvement scale is to be used with reference to the involvement signals.

Level 1 Low activity: stereotypic, repetitive and passive, with little effort or indication that the child feels that much is demanded. They are easily distracted, after which the activity is forgotten.

Level 2 A frequently interrupted activity: the child is engaged in an activity for part of the time, but spends approximately half of the observed period not paying direct attention. They are relatively easily distracted, after which the activity is forgotten.

Level 3 Mainly continuous activity: the child seems busy at an activity but there is the feeling that 'something' is lacking and that the task is routine. They are relatively easily distracted, and may not return to the activity.

Level 4 Continuous activity with intense moments: there are some signs of intensity in the child's engagement. They can be interrupted, but not wholly distracted, seeking out and resuming the activity again following the interruption. They may resist interruption in some cases. Attention may fluctuate a little, but in general there is high concentration and focus.

Level 5 Sustained intense activity: the child shows concentration, creativity, energy and persistence for almost all the observation period. They show little response to interruptions, and have clear motivation to continue the activity.

The authors suggest that such observations be carried out via the time-sampling method, observing a child for two minutes.

The ECERS (Early Childhood Environment Rating Scales)

ECERS-R is based on seven subscales:

- Space and furnishings

- Personal care routines

- Language reasoning

- Activities

- Interaction

- Programme structure

- Parents and staff

ECERS-E is based on four subscales:

- Literacy

- Mathematics

- Science and environment

- Diversity

These aspects are scored along a continuum

1	2	3	4	5	6	7

Inadequate   Minimal   Good   Excellent

The scales are used as follows:

1 = Inadequate

- Children's needs for health and safety are not met
- No warmth or support from adults is observed
- No learning is encouraged

3 = Minimal

- Children's basic health and safety needs are met
- A little warmth and support is provided by adults
- There are few learning experiences

5 = Good

- Health and safety needs are fully met
- Staff are caring and supportive of children
- Children are learning in many ways through interesting, fun activities

7 = Excellent

- Everything is good
- In addition, children are encouraged to become independent
- The teacher plans for children's individual learning needs
- Adults have close, personal relationships with each child

The ITERS-R (Infant-Toddler Environment Rating Scale, Revised) has seven subscales, each of which yield a scale score, using the same scoring system as ECERS. The subscales are:

I   Space and furnishings:

   1   Indoor space

   2   Furniture for routine care and play

   3   Provision for relaxation and comfort

   4   Room arrangement

   5   Display for children

II   Personal care routines:

6   Greeting/departing

7   Meals/snacks

8   Nap

9   Nappy changing/toileting

10   Health practices

11   Safety practices

III   Listening and talking:

12   Helping children understand language

13   Helping children use language

14   Using books

IV   Activities:

15   Fine motor

16   Active physical play

17   Art

18   Music and movement

19   Blocks

20   Dramatic play

21   Sand and water play

22   Nature/science

23   Use of TV, video and/or computer

24   Promoting acceptance of diversity

V   Interaction:

25   Supervision of play and learning

26   Peer interaction

27   Staff-child interaction

28   Discipline

VI Programme structure:

29 Schedule

30 Free play

31 Group play activities

32 Provisions for children with disabilities

VII Parents and staff

33 Provisions for parents

34 Provisions for personal needs of staff

35 Provisions for professional needs of staff

36 Staff interaction and co-operation

37 Staff continuity

38 Supervision and evaluation of staff

39 Opportunities for professional growth

(ECERS and ITERS outline above based on information in Harms et al. 2006)

It is likely that student researchers will 'dip' into these methods, using them for the purposes of their research topic; for example, Ellie might find the personal care routines and interaction categories of ECERS-R quite useful for her study of the key person in her setting, while the other categories will not match her focus. Sunil on the other hand may find the whole of the Leuven Scale quite useful, depending upon the detail in the data that he collects.

Meeting methodological requirements

Observation is a very versatile method in which it is possible to collect a range of qualitative and quantitative data – all observation methods produce snippets of qualitative data such as quotes (especially from children) that can add detail and colour to data from questionnaires and surveys. You may also choose to use a fairly light touch in your observational data if you additionally have some detailed interview data to analyse. On the other hand, it is quite possible to carry out extensive thematic analysis and coding of observational data if you have carried out detailed observations as the principal method for your investigation. Where you have carried out a quantitative observational method, you should find that you have some useful data to display in tables, graphs and charts (see Chapter 7), which can be summarised and further analysed using descriptive statistics.

You should find that using tried and tested observation methods will help you to produce reliable results, but, as outlined above, you will have to observe and record objectively and in sufficient detail, particularly where 'thick description' data is required. You will need to take special care with identifying themes and coding observations; these are judgements that you will make based on what you have observed (see below).

Your skills in observing and recording objectively will of course also influence the validity of the results. You will need to remain unobtrusive at all times, and may need to cease observing and devise an alternative plan if the observed participants and their behaviour are being affected by your presence. You will also need to take special care in participant observations not to 'lead' your participants, whether child or adult.

Representativeness: reliability, validity and generalisability in observational research

In order to ensure representativeness you need to be sure that the participants of your observations represent the 'set' you are investigating. You will need to have a plan for a sample of participants that are representative of the group you wish to study.

Sunil

. . . contemplates the potential reliability and validity of his data. He considers that, if he is trying to collect data to inform a research question focusing upon boys' learning through play, it will not be possible to observe all of the boys at play in his class - so will this affect the reliability of his data? He could select a random sample of boys to observe, but what if that doesn't turn out to be representative of the whole group, e.g. age group, ethnicity? He is also beginning to realise that if he were to decide to observe the boys who are most likely to take part in outdoor play (and, he reflects, one or two of the girls) it is likely that these will be the more boisterous, active children and the results will be skewed away from the children who

▶

take more part in indoor activities, and consequently have less time to spend outdoors. He discusses his worries with his tutor who refocuses him on the point that his key questions revolved around: how to interest the most reluctant readers in purposive pre-literacy activities designed for the outdoor area. 'All student research is a pilot to some extent', she advises him. 'As long as you recognise the problems that you are beginning to identify in your write-up, you won't be penalised; this will only happen if you study a small group of children in one setting and then imply (or even claim!) that your findings are key to designing pre-literacy activities for all boys, everywhere.' Sunil walks away thinking that, when it is explained to him like this, it all seems very simple, but when he cannot directly ask questions of this nature things go round and round and round in his head. . . .

Reflection point

The 'things going round in your head' feeling is very common in the undergraduate dissertation student experience. Do, like Sunil, make good use of your tutor, but don't forget that discussion with other students can also be helpful, either face to face or through IT portals (e.g. college forums, email or Facebook). Do remember however to be discreet about the material that you share and the comments that you make, as once sent these may stay where they are sent for a very long time, and be read by people that you did not intend to see them (see Chapter 2).

Observations have a really useful role to play in triangulating the findings from questionnaires and surveys, due to the 'real life' nature of the method, as outlined above. Where the data is 'thick' enough to thematicise, this is particularly the case.

Nick

. . . contemplates that, having started out as a convinced positivist, he is now looking at the prospect of gathering almost exclusively qualitative data. He is going to use the 'focus area' technique, trying to produce 'thick description' of the children's use of his maths activities. He will then interview his TAs to compare whether their understandings of what the children were doing, and

▶

whether their evaluations of the success (or not) of the activities match his own. He reflects that, particularly given his earlier problems with his relationship with his TAs, they might still be inclined to tell him what he wants to hear rather than what they really think. He discusses this with his tutor, who agrees that this is a problem, but whatever happens, the relationship between the observations and the interviews will inevitably generate ideas for the discussion section of his report. She advises him to 'stop trying to control everything, and open yourself up to what the data is telling you'. Nick finds himself thinking that this is beginning to sound like a yoga class (or even a counselling session), but walking away he reflects that he *has* always found it very difficult to relax in activities in which he feels that he does not have a clear view of the eventual end result.

Reflection point

This is another very common feeling at the 'creating the methodology' stage of your research. Nick is not unusual in finding the type of uncertainty attached to social research activity quite unnerving. Like Sunil, he might also benefit from discussing these feelings with other students, if only to discover that he is not alone in his concerns.

Creating themes in observational data

The most typical data used for thematic analysis in Early Years education and care research is drawn from narrative observations where 'thick description' of activities and interactions has been generated. It is not uncommon when sitting down with several pages of observational transcript to feel quite overwhelmed and unable to 'make sense' of such a large amount of material. The best way to start is to read the script carefully through once, without making any marks at all on the paper. Once you have finished, read through several more times, making notes on the script about anything interesting or significant. You may also try to summarise some of your comments, if you find them getting rather lengthy, or even some of the content of the script. It is traditional to make these notes in the right-hand margin, but you can do this in any way that you feel comfortable. However you format this, your initial notes should be in *the relevant area of the script,* not on a separate sheet, so make sure to leave large margins and use double-line spacing on observation transcripts. If you stray away from the raw data at this point, you may begin to lose focus, so it is important that you make a concerted effort to stay with the observation transcript.

It is often best to finish a study session when you feel you cannot make any more notes on a particular script. Then when you return for a subsequent session, first of all read your notes back (not the script). Do some 'themes' begin to arise; i.e. key words that capture the intuitive essence of what is recorded in the script? It is traditional to note these in the left-hand margin of the script. Now return to the script and check that these 'key words' do indeed reflect what is recorded there. It is common to find that some do, and some don't. Focusing upon the ones that do, and deleting those that don't, list emerging themes and look for possible connections between them; two or three themes are usual for a detailed observation transcript. Note these connections on a separate sheet of paper, and add an accompanying memo that describes the scope of each theme.

Move on to the next observation script and carry out the same process. You will begin to see where each script is highly individual (a theme or themes that only emerge from that observation) and where there are similarities (a theme or themes that are found in several observations). You may also find patterns in themes in that they correspond to the demographic categories of the participants, e.g. male/female, older/younger. Given human variability, it is unusual to find the same set of themes in every observation script in the batch that you have created regardless of gender/age. You will inevitably find that some participants follow the trends that you identify among alternative demographic groups, for example girls who prefer to play outside with the boys, and older people who are highly positive about new innovations.

Themes will expand, contract or change as you analyse more transcripts. This is perfectly normal. You should end up with key themes that describe the essence of your data, in terms of those that you find are most common, and some useful 'discussion' themes that emerge strongly from one or two scripts but are not present in the others. As indicated in Chapter 4, you can use exactly the same technique to draw themes from scripted semi-structured or unstructured interviews.

It is common to present findings and analysis together when analysing thematic data, using the themes as headings. You then explain the content of the theme (using your 'memos') and present some examples from the scripts to illustrate the material that caused you to generate the theme in question.

Florentyna

. . . has not yet finished her data collection, but she has decided to start practising the creation of some themes from her existing data. She finds in her observations that children are more likely to generate original play in her forest area than in the other areas of the setting; that they persevere more with problem solving where things do not go as they expect, and that they are more likely to engage in co-operative problem solving. She has a range of examples to illustrate, for example:

Jenny showed Isma the 'fairy ring' under the tree-stump. Isma then called to Reehana and Suzie to come and look. The girls then sat down and talked about fairies for five minutes, and the next day Suzie brought in a book of fairies dancing around a ring just like the one in the forest area.

Tom, Jonny and Atul played at superheroes for nearly half an hour, making up a story about a burglar (or burg-u-lar!) they had to catch before he stole (or 'dog-napped') Emily's puppy.

As you can see, Florentyna has some examples of the children's language associated with these activities that she can use in her final report. She also has some data that have emerged from her Mosaic method, which, while not being strictly 'observational', provide excellent supporting evidence – for example, Tom's fuzzy photo of Jonny being Batman, and Suzie's drawing of her favourite part of the forest area – the fairy ring.

Reflection point

Of course, Florentyna will not include Tom's photo of Jonny in her write-up; this has gone into Jonny's profile, with Tom's permission. It is wise of Florentyna to start contemplating her themes quite early in the process; as you are probably beginning to realise, this type of 'deep' analysis is not something that can be accomplished in one quick session when you are stressed and desperate for 'results'. However, it is worth persevering, as it is within such activities that the deepest levels of understanding are built.

Conclusion

As this chapter comes to an end, you may be thinking that observation sounds rather complex, but when you get 'into' your methodology you will find that it is not as difficult as it may appear. It is definitely worth persevering with this method if you are a practitioner student in an Early Years education and care setting, as it is the one in which you will learn the most about the children. In the short term, this will obviously help towards a good mark for your dissertation, but don't forget the long term. You will emerge as a more skilled and thoughtful practitioner, with many more 'strings to your bow' with respect to designing activities that will both excite and educate the children with whom you will work, and you will be able to call upon these for the whole extent of your future career.

References

David, M., Edwards, R. and Alldred, P. (2001) Children and School-Based Research: Informed Consent or Educated Consent?, *British Educational Research Journal*, 27 (3): 141–92.

DfES Standards Unit (2005) *Health and Social Care*: https://www.education.gov.uk/publications/eOrderingDownload/SUNA04.pdf [accessed 5 November 2011].

Harms, T., Cryer, D. and Clifford, R.M. (2006) *Infant/Toddler Environment Rating Scale, Revised Edition Manual*, New York: Teachers College Press.

Hobart, C. and Frankel, J. (1994) *A Practical Guide to Child Observation*, Cheltenham: Stanley Thornes.

Laevers, F. (1994) *The Leuven Involvement Scale for Young Children*, Leuven, Belgium: Centre for Experiential Education.

Palaiologou, I. (2008) *Childhood Observation*, Exeter: Learning Matters.

Pascal, C. and Bertram, A.D. (1997) *Effective Early Learning: Case Studies of Improvement*, London: Hodder and Stoughton.

Riddall-Leech, S. (2008) *How to Observe Children*, Harlow: Heinemann.

Sylva, K., Roy, C. and Painter, M. (1986) *Childwatching at Playgroup and Nursery School*, Oxford: Blackwell.

Chapter 6
Putting research methods into action

Wendy Holland and Pam Jarvis

Introduction

This chapter will take you through four different examples that illustrate how research may unfold in practice for students in Early Years/education. We are going to follow Nick, Ellie, Florentyna and Sunil as they move through their practical research, implementing their methodologies and responding to issues that arise. We will also consider some of the impacts that their investigations have upon their day-to-day practice, some that they would have had great difficulty in predicting. No doubt you, too, will find this to be an interesting and maybe even sometimes surprising and perplexing feature of research carried out within a working environment; perhaps some of your experiences may mirror those you will find outlined below.

Nick

Nick was beginning to reflect that, in Early Years practice, subject knowledge could sometimes prove a bit of a barrier to effective practice. It had already led him to over-expect what the TAs should be doing with the children in his reception class, and as he tried to devise some 'fun' mathematical activities he kept having to refer to the EYFS guidance on Problem Solving Reasoning and Numeracy for 40–60+ months, to ensure the games and activities he was attempting to create were developmentally appropriate. He wished he'd paid more attention in the Child Development lectures, but, if he was honest, he'd sometimes felt himself at odds with ideas that had been discussed in some of the sessions at college. Surely we'd moved on from nineteenth-century theories which seemed to be increasingly challenged by contemporary research; what did they really have to do with life in the classroom? He 'got' Vygotsky; from a teaching perspective that made a lot of sense – the more knowledgeable adult helping a child to take the next step in their understanding. That's what he wanted to achieve with his activities. He also knew, from observing children at first hand, that structured play could help create such moments.

His predecessor in the reception class (a recently retired Miss Jones) had favoured a more formal approach to teaching mathematics, relying more on the Numeracy Strategies in the National Curriculum, adapting these for the younger children. She had also left several boxes of commercially produced worksheets behind, that Nick had had to throw out in order to clear himself some cupboard space when he first took over the class.

Nick had guessed from the lacklustre displays of children's number-work that, as with the TAs, mathematics had not been her favourite subject. He thought back to his literature review, recalling several pieces of research that highlighted the lack of enthusiasm for numeracy among female Early Years practitioners. He was back to his concern again, how to prevent the stereotype of maths being 'hard' as well as 'dull' and 'for boys'. He recalled his research question (it was imprinted in his brain now): the activities had to be *relevant* and *flexible*, reflecting the *individual interests* of children, as well as helping them to work towards the Early Learning Goals for Problem Solving Reasoning and Numeracy (PSRN). He recalled a small group of girls, earlier in the week, who, during their choosing time, had taken over the home corner and practised being brides and bridesmaids. One of the mothers had brought in an old bridal gown, cut down to size, and another some second-hand bridesmaids' dresses. It wasn't surprising, Nick reflected, when the TV, newspapers and magazines were full of photographs and articles about the impending royal wedding. Some of these too had found their way into the home corner. Nick hadn't really got involved with it, but he had noticed the positive impact upon the communication skills among the group. He'd asked one of the TAs to do an observation for the girls' profiles. He considered for a moment how he might use this current interest to support some 'fun' mathematical activities. 'Make it into a bridal shop', his partner suggested during one of their rare evening meals together. 'They could measure the princess for her wedding dress.' Nick looked at her a little nervously and wondered if 'wedding fever' was catching. Nevertheless, it was a good idea.

The next morning, after register, he talked to the children about his ideas. 'Nooo!', groaned some of the boys. 'But we'd have special uniforms, too, for the soldiers', his TA encouraged, 'like the guards wear at Buckingham Palace.' Later that day Nick put a note on the parents' board, asking for resources for the project, after which all manner of props and accessories, from outgrown 'prom' dresses to plastic tiaras and top hats, poured in, even a battered old cash register that beeped and churned out receipts. Once it was set up, he and Diane, his regular TA, modelled being shopkeeper and customer, rather self-consciously on Nick's part, he reflected. The opportunities for recognising numbers, shapes, counting 'change', solving problems through the use of mathematical language were many: How much paper did it take to wrap a pair of lacy white gloves? Did it take more to wrap a wide-brimmed hat? Did Sajid need a bigger jacket than Tom? Was Kirsty's veil longer than Sophie's? Which was heavier, Josie's bouquet or Kim's? Diane, a particularly creative TA (who was also not at all self-conscious in active role play), had made brightly coloured labels and price tags, using a combination of pictures, symbols and words, as well as Union Jack flags.

Nick wrote some prompts designed to explore mathematical understanding, using appropriate language, displaying them on the wall by the shop for practitioners to use when engaging in the bridal shop role play, and waited a couple of days before he began his observations. He wondered briefly about the ethics of this, but decided that as he wasn't directly questioning the children, and observing children for their individual profiles was accepted practice, he didn't think there would be any real issues. He'd decided on doing non-participant observations, using hand-written notes. He liked the idea of using some type of recording device too, but when he suggested this to his tutor she reminded him about gaining 'informed consent'. So he talked to the children at circle time. One of the four-year-olds, Josie, who had immediately made good of the bridal shop, was keen to know, 'Will it be like – like a real princess on the telly?' Diane, the TA (who tended to have favourites, Nick had noticed), was tying up the frayed ribbon on Josie's hair (lice free this week), as if preparing her for an audition. 'No', Nick explained, 'I'm not using the video camera, just recording your voices, if that's alright with you?' The children nodded in unison, one of the boys asking, 'Can we listen to how we sound?'

Nick re-read the rules on his dissertation module booklet, and consequently decided to send a letter home explaining to parents what he planned to do, and giving them the right to withdraw their child, if they so wished. There were no complaints; in fact, the one or two supportive parents he knew he could rely on were pleased and curious, asking to be kept informed of his findings. Nick, knowing they had the right to be kept informed, agreed, at the same time hoping his 'findings' would have a positive outcome.

If the TAs did their job properly, Nick felt he could manage to record some significant responses linked to individual children's use and understanding of numeracy. His first observation session went well. He'd planned to do it ten minutes before tidy-up time prior to lunch. He reflected afterwards on how well Diane had used his prompts and engaged in some quality sustained shared thinking around PSRN with individual children, as well as being good at managing the group's behaviour (one or two arguments over who was going to be the bride first had erupted, and a couple of the boys wearing dress uniforms had manufactured 'swords' from cardboard tubes at the Design and Technology table, wanting to play fight).

When it came to transcribing his recording, however, Nick was disappointed to find that the general noise levels in the room had almost drowned out the children's voices. He tried 'filling in the gaps' from his brief notes, but unfortunately he'd kept getting distracted by children asking him what he was doing, and Samira had even pulled up a chair and, note book in hand, copied Nick's every move, proudly telling everyone, 'I'm a researcher like Sir!' Nick contemplated sadly that what he was left with didn't adequately reflect the rich activity that he had observed. He gave up trying to make sense of it and decided to begin again at the next opportunity using a different method. Two days later he planned another observation using a check-list proforma he used when observing the children for their profile information. He'd doctored it a little by only using descriptors from the profile assessment scales for PSRN. It was a different TA today, Claire, who seemed eager to help Nick with his research. She normally supported Peter, a four-year-old boy thought to be on the autistic spectrum, but he hadn't arrived this particular morning. Nick noticed how different she was from Diane, tending to dominate and control the children's play, bombarding them with closed questions, additionally dressing up in some of the accessories, a plastic tiara and feather boa, and telling them, 'I'm Princess Di'!

'Who?' said Kirsty to Sophie, who replied with a puzzled shrug. The numbers quickly dwindled, then five minutes into the observation the teacher on outdoor duty brought in two boys who had come to blows over a football. 'Miss, my head hurts', gulped the smaller boy, while the slightly older, more stocky child, surreptitiously kneed him in the back of the leg. Claire automatically stopped what she was doing and went to help with the situation, tiara and boa intact. At this point, Nick wished he'd gone with his initial idea of providing his older group with table tasks and number games, with himself as a participant observer. But when he'd suggested this to his tutor, she had asked him to reflect upon whether that approach would meet his own criteria of 'interesting and flexible'.

Nick persevered with his observations over a three-week period using a mixture of note-taking and check-list, which he began to convert specifically to suit his particular style and the material available. He had to change the focus during the last week, as the novelty of the brides' shop had begun to wane, especially with the boys, frustrated that their rough and tumble play was not welcome by the girls in such a *haute couture* environment, and the quarrels that developed resulted in the increasingly elaborate swords and light sabres being frequently confiscated. Nick brought out a large squared number mat he'd ordered at the beginning of term, which had remained stored in its wrapper, together with a huge numbered die. This proved to be a less markedly 'gendered' activity; both the girls and boys clearly enjoyed the 'active' element of the game, and, with TAs using the prompts he provided, it resulted in some really clear indications of the children's skills round ordinal and cardinal numbering and number bonds to 10. He wondered if he had enough material from all his notes, check-lists and recordings to support some kind of detailed analysis. Time seemed to be leaching away. Nick decided what he had managed to gather so far (a well-filled notebook and a substantial sheaf of check-lists, he reflected, despite his earlier misgivings) would have to suffice for the observational part of the method. He still had to design structured interviews to use with the TAs, if he was going to successfully triangulate his data.

He decided to manage the interviews more ethically than his abortive early questionnaire, doing everything by the book, talking with the TAs about the purposes of his research, giving them the opportunity to withdraw, promising them confidentiality and anonymity and access to his results. He phoned his tutor to discuss the interviews, and in the same phone call they decided that he should rely on this method for his triangulation and not send questionnaires home to the parents, given the likelihood that they would meet with the same fate as his earlier questionnaires to the TAs.

Nick re-read the information given on the use of interviewing as a procedure, and pondered over which format would best suit his purposes, given his time constraints. He'd come to accept that an interpretivist approach would provide better quality data when researching the behaviour of children and adults. His tutor had emphasised this in her tutorial, indicating that the advantage of semi-structured or unstructured interviews was that they would provide 'rich' data, the disadvantage being that they took longer to analyse. He'd already set himself the tedious task of transcribing the observation recording, and time was pressing. He felt that structured interviews would be easier to control and categorise. He reasoned the TAs would probably prefer that anyway, then in a moment of honest reflection admitted *he* would feel more confident asking structured questions.

Half-term wasn't far away and he'd planned to use this break to sort out his data, which meant there was simply no time to do a pilot study. He discussed his structured interview questions with his tutor. 'This seems fine, Nick, but in terms of the data you'll collect – well, you could just as easily have used a questionnaire.' Nick felt a little deflated. He also found that designing an effective questionnaire could not be rushed. He'd always prided himself on his own use of language, debunking the stereotype of 'science and maths people not being very good with words'. He'd often been commended in his previous job for his succinct and readable reports. It was the rules surrounding the construction of a questionnaire that were beginning to confound him. If only he'd allowed himself more time. The more he struggled, the less confident he became. There was also the tricky issue of value-laden words, closed questions, leading questions, ambiguous phrases – Nick got to the point where he wondered how any questionnaires saw the light of day!

Reflection point

If you were Nick, how would you proceed now? In the end, Nick rang his tutor to discuss and it was agreed between them that he would undertake 15-minute semi-structured interviews with the TAs using three direct prompts as follows:

- Do you think there are any barriers to the idea of 'maths' among adults working in Early Years classrooms? (With follow-up prompts to help interviewees explain/expand upon any barriers that they identify)

- What is your own evaluation of the activities we have used this term to try to make maths more fun? (With follow-up to help explanation/expansion on comments arising)

- How do you think we should build on these activities next term?

'What if they go on and on and on, or their ideas are completely illogical, or they go completely off the point?', Nick asked. 'How do you deal with this type of situation in the everyday classroom?', his tutor responds. Nick thought for a moment, and said, 'Oh, I am beginning to see . . . and I could use the classroom timer to time the interviews, couldn't I?' He discussed this with his partner after watching Jeremy Paxman on *Newsnight* raised some follow-up thoughts about conducting a succinct interview. His partner smiled at him and said, 'But remember to be a bit more gentle with them, dear – they are not international politicians after all.' Nick smiled back, while at the same time making a more serious mental note to 'keep it relaxed'!

Ellie

Ellie realised how her tutor had helped her reflect upon her initial perspective, a positivist 'here's the solution – let's implement it' approach, and how it had changed through her readings to a more interpretivist one. The idea of Action Research, although a 'slower solution' to the 'problem' her manager, Alice, had asked to her address, now really did seem the best option. She only hoped any small changes she was planning to introduce would satisfy Alice, or at least buy
Ellie more time. Hopefully, Ellie might persuade Alice that small steps were best when expecting staff to change their practice. Alice clearly most valued structure and order, praising some practitioners over others for their carefully ordered and planned rooms, so the initial action plan Ellie had created at the beginning of her research had won Alice's approval, with its simple, measured, achievable, relevant and timed structure. But that had been before Ellie had realised the complexities of the task she'd been set, when her clearer 'positivistic' approach had supported easier solutions. Her reading and research had helped her understand that the initial solution she had introduced, of allowing each child's preference to dictate their key person, in itself had not been such a bad idea, reflecting as it did (although she had not been aware of it at the time) some of the literature and research on attachment. The problem, she now realised, had been its impact on accepted practice in the setting. Ellie was sure of one thing: whatever action she took now, she would need to get the staff's agreement for it to stand any real chance of success.

Ellie thought back to how she had prepared the staff before introducing the 'child preference' changes to key person practice, and realised now, with her wider perspectives on attachment, that she had relied on the brief training the staff had been given on the role of the key person as part of the EYFS statutory requirement. She now accepted that this was too narrow, and decided to do some further staff training on the role of the key person – and a modified view of its relationship to attachment – at the next staff meeting. She also thought it would be a good opportunity to introduce one of the 'small changes' to practice she had been thinking about at the same time. This involved assigning an 'understudy' in each room, who could take over when the key person was absent. If she ended the session asking staff to complete a short response/ satisfaction sheet before they left, this would provide her immediately with initial data that could be triangulated with interviews of staff after the new changes had been in practice for a few weeks.

Ellie discussed this modified action plan with her tutor, adding that the data from interviews would be analysed and used to create further 'acceptable' small changes, which could then be tested against staff opinions. Using this cyclical approach, Ellie hoped, would result in a solution to the key person role that all practitioners would be happy with. She'd need to 'sell' the idea to her manager, and the area manager, both of whom were expecting minor miracles within a very short space of time, in particular orderly, organised change. Hopefully, by keeping them informed, showing them the positive and progressive results from each small change as it was embedded into daily practice would provide her with room for manoeuvre and the time she needed to finish her research.

Her tutor pointed out, 'You need to be careful not to prejudge the outcomes of the changes, Ellie, and they may not be the ones you expect. Try to remain objective; that way you will handle your data with a more open mind.' She also reminded Ellie of the need to justify her choice of procedures, reinforcing the positives and negatives of using interviews as a means of gathering data. The awkward question of objectivity was also raised again. Ellie realised her tutor was trying to politely suggest she was being drawn into addressing the needs of the setting, at the expense of her research project, and that she needed to redress the balance between work needs and research. However, Ellie knew that, if she went too far along the 'I'm doing research' line, her managers would remind her who was giving her paid day release for her studies . . . she sighed.

Although she hadn't voiced it, the reason Ellie had quickly dismissed the idea of using questionnaires had more to do with Alice's reluctance to her handing them out to staff (if the parents found out – and one parent was a part-time member of staff – they might think that the management of the setting didn't know what they were doing!) than with the complexities of designing a questionnaire with its rules about ambiguity, bias, double-barrelled questions, and quantification, to name but a few! She'd read somewhere that practitioner researchers had 'power', so why did she feel so powerless?

Ellie decided that she needed to think positively (not positivistically!) and make a choice on the type of interview she would use, after the understudies approach had been trialled. Her tutor suggested that structured interviews might not provide such 'rich' data as semi- or unstructured interviews. Knowing her intended interviewees and their capacity to talk at length on most subjects, Ellie opted for a semi-structured approach. That way she would have some 'control' over the discussion, as well as gaining ideas of what they really felt. There had been a lot of 'rumblings' among staff at her previous failed attempt to 'impose' a solution, and the last thing she wanted was a repeat performance. She knew getting to the bottom of 'why' practitioners felt in a particular way about the key person role, as well as her latest innovation, was the answer to creating good practice and a workable key person policy. She needed to respect whatever views the data presented and seriously consider any changes to practice it might suggest, even if they were at odds with her own ideas. This was where it became so difficult to be an 'objective' practitioner and researcher, remaining unbiased, when the outcomes could affect everyone's working practice on a daily basis, especially her own.

She recalled the 'tips' given about organising successful interviews. The sensory room immediately came to mind. Out of the way and in the process of being revamped (after recommendations from the last OfSTED inspector), it meant they wouldn't be disturbed. The interviews themselves needed to be evenly timed, though she knew some members of staff felt more strongly about this issue than others. Recalling and recording staff responses, Ellie didn't think that would be a problem. She had confidence in her ability to memorise - years of remembering observations of children for their profiles had honed that particular skill - and the staff wouldn't be distracted if she made the odd note; note-taking on post-its was standard practice. Organising the rota to allow time for fair coverage of the interviews would, however, be a headache; she would need to get the manager on board to give cover in the rooms.

The best laid plans, Ellie thought ruefully, after she had conducted a pilot of the interview questions. It wasn't so much the questions themselves (they only needed a few tweaks), but the process of interviewing, recalling and recording had raised unexpected issues. Writing on post-its, it turned out, was not the best option for her, and remembering an interview in detail, even a short one, was a lot more complicated than making observations of children during their play. She had ended up with gaps in the conversations and scribbled notes, which, because of staff absences, she hadn't been able to revisit for several days, after which they looked as if they'd been written in a foreign language. She made a mental note to search out some type of recording device before the interviews proper began. Trying to remain positive, she realised there was a plus point in that ethical considerations would not be an issue. Her manager had given consent for the project, anxious for something practical to come out of it. The staff, too, had been unanimous in wanting the research to begin and finish as soon as possible. Ellie picked up on a comment from one of the practitioners that, until the issues around the key person role had been resolved, practitioners, children and parents alike were 'being short-changed'.

Her original timed action plan seemed almost laughable in the light of 'real' time. Some things she couldn't have factored in, like her eldest daughter fracturing several fingers on her right hand. Ellie tried to be supportive and sympathetic, but every day simple things, like getting everyone ready in the morning, took that bit longer. Plus, she'd had to cope with pressure from the management over the cost of providing cover for the staff interviews that she had planned to start the following week. Ellie began to wonder if they were really necessary. Initial 'anecdotal' responses to the 'understudy' changes were already looking positive. The change had created a more flexible approach among staff, less 'possessiveness' among key workers, and wider sets of staff observations of children and increased general involvement with them. Ellie recalled a practitioner's remark, expressing concerns in the absence of their key worker of children being in 'no-man's land'. This had certainly been addressed by the understudy arrangement. She briefly toyed with the idea of relying on this anecdotal data, but soon dismissed it. How could that help to triangulate anything? She was swiftly brought back to 'reality' by a parent complaining: 'I don't like this idea of Lucy having two key people, it's confusing for her – and me! I much preferred it when it was just us and Sharon. I've nothing against Aisha personally; I just don't feel I can confide in the same way.' Ellie knew this particular parent had developed what she now realised was a rather over-close relationship with her child's key worker, and resented having to liaise with someone else. She made a mental note that, in spite of her manager's opposition to involving parents, their views (and this had been confirmed in the literature) were just as important. This was something she could think about when this first round of interviews had been completed.

Ellie used a revised list of questions from the pilot study, ranging from more general questions about what practitioners thought of the *idea* of the key person role itself, the impact, if any, of the new government review of the Early Years guidelines upon the key person role; to more specific questions such as what they thought of the current trialled use of 'understudies' and what changes, if any, they'd like to see to the key person role. To ensure reliability, she kept generally to the same format for each interview, regardless of the practitioner's role within the setting. Recording the interviews was initially so much better, but when it came to transcribing she realised all the warnings she had been given about the length of time it took to handle such qualitative data (and which she had dismissed as a bit ridiculous) were indeed true.

She began by using a **themed** analysis, a bit like the approach used in her literature review where the terms **bonding, attachment, settling in, responsibilities, parental preferences** were all key words and phrases that emerged from her electronic word search. Ellie soon realised just how strongly the majority of the staff felt about the key worker issue, finding that most of the themes she was generating related to feeling unsure of boundaries (e.g. how do I respond to another person's key child if they are not present?) and uncertainty about their own skills as a key worker (e.g. 'Jasmine cried and cried until Angie picked her up and sang to her – I'm supposed to be her key worker, but she wouldn't let me comfort her'). Ellie had previously thought, judging from the answers she'd received on the training response sheets, it was only those members of staff who held key person posts who had strong views, but it soon became apparent this was an issue upon which all the staff had a considered opinion, and the use of understudies had brought it to the surface. Ellie wondered if it reflected an unvoiced concern that related directly to her research question: 'To what extent *can* the key person address young children's needs for a **bonded relationship** within a **collective care** setting?' Had her staff training on the complexities of attachment and the key person role resulted in a more interpretivistic approach among the *staff*? Ellie realised she was speculating, and went back to looking at the actual data.

She tried really hard to see it objectively, but couldn't help 'rationalising' some of the responses from people she had worked with for some time now. It had come as no surprise to see the room leader for the 0–2s being very positive about the need for a more flexible interpretation of the key worker role, and applauding the use of understudies, of which she felt there should be more, adding that, '*This is a complaint I have generally against the key person system. Giving one person sole responsibility for a child has the effect of making other practitioners "back off" from accepting responsibility for a child; the understudy approach at least prevents a child being "in no-man's land".*' Hearing the phrase again stirred Ellie's memory into recalling her journal entry about young Katie's unsettled day and her mother's anxiety when she had come to collect her. Ellie did not want to find blame, but had other practitioners been 'casual' in their dealings with the child? Had the child picked up on a subconscious feeling of 'it's not my responsibility' on the part of the staff who had attempted to comfort her? It was too long ago now to recall accurately. She wished her journal entry had been more detailed at the time.

The room leader for the 3-5 year-olds, who had previously worked for many years as a nursery nurse in a local authority nursery school, felt they should be reflecting more what happened in local nurseries and reception classes with the older children; there the key person's role was 'played down' and it was *more a collective thing - in reception it's all down to the teacher' - 'I don't think older children or their parents need that "one to one" so much, as long as you talk with them regularly, keep them informed.'*

Several staff felt the understudies trial still didn't address the real problems, suggesting there should be a 'settling-in time' followed by parental preferences for their child's key person, their rationale for this being that parents knew their children better than staff. One of the staff who suggested this, however, felt it could lead to similar problems around unfair workloads that had occurred when they'd trialled child preferences.

Ellie felt her head was spinning after the interviews; she'd anticipated some diverse views would emerge, but it was the strength of feeling that had surprised her. Whatever the research finally showed, she had to address practice and get it right. It was so difficult to remain separate from the data. Part of her wished she'd gone down a more quantitative route. Her next tutorial reminded her that she had to triangulate her findings, and at this point she decided that she would do this with a very simple questionnaire to parents, just checking on how they felt that the key person system was working. She had previously managed to sneak this past Alice as a Quality Assurance measure that would be positively viewed in the next OfSTED inspection.

Then, work at the setting became so hectic as they got ready for an early Easter, there were simply not enough hours in the day, and, with two members of staff off with 'flu' to cover for, her research took a back seat. Almost two weeks went by before Ellie looked at her interview data again. Time away from it, however, provided more clarity; she could now see how, small scale as it may be, several of the themes from her literature review were echoed in the staff's responses, for example the acknowledgement of the importance of attachment in a young child's life, the need for parents to be involved, the impact of multiple relationships within organised daycare. This finding was also echoed in her questionnaire to parents, where the main concerns emerged as the child 'being happy' in the setting, and knowing who they should 'talk to' if they had any concerns. So far so good, thought Ellie.

Florentyna

Florentyna decided to create a 'target area' proforma that involved the six areas of learning, her reasoning being the more evidence she could provide for coverage of the six areas, the better she might persuade some of the more sceptical members of staff to reflect on their own practice. She decided on non-participatory observations, as these would help her see the bigger picture necessary to track the range of activities the children were involved in during their forest school sessions. She liked the idea of the mosaic approach because of its inherent creativity. Some self-assessment by the children was already common practice in the setting, but it generally involved a child pointing to where they thought they might be on a cardboard caterpillar with its segments numbered, together with some questioning of why that was. She thought the use of photographs and drawings/paintings by the children so much more relevant, part of the 'hundred languages' children naturally used.

The digital cameras were normally used by the adults and only in special circumstances by the children, usually with an adult present (in case of damage). It would take real persuasion to let the children 'loose' with them in the 'forest', and Florentyna only achieved it by virtually promising to remedy any breakages or damage. It was worth it. The results were really great. Among the collection of cut-off heads and legs, unfocused action shots and pictures of grass, there were real gems. Sally had focused on a snail clinging to some bark; Paul, the pattern of shadows made by the leaves through sunlight. Jenny had gone looking for the 'homes' of fairies from the fairy ring, and was convinced they lived under some (harmless) fungi at the root of a tree stump, while Tom had taken several fuzzy photographs of his friends being superheroes, jumping off logs into the dust or puddles. These child authored photographs clearly revealed their perceptions and interests.

Florentyna felt she had made some kind of breakthrough, when the deputy manager asked if she could put the photographs on a loop in the entrance for parents to look at. Florentyna had no hesitation in saying yes. The responses to the photographs had been a little mixed, one or two parents commenting on 'safety issues', a few others complaining of 'dirty' children and 'dirty' clothes after forest school sessions, but overall Florentyna felt responses had been positive.

The pilot study for her staff questionnaire, however, was not a success. It revealed real differences in 'philosophy' among staff about unstructured play generally, and risk assessment in particular. Florentyna was distressed to hear several staff commenting that they'd felt 'on trial' during the pilot. She had been praised for her 'insightful' and 'relevant' questions by her tutor. Had it been her delivery, her body language? She felt genuinely at a loss. When the deputy manager decided to put the issue on the agenda for the following week's staff meeting, things went from bad to worse. Through her literature searches, Florentyna had come across a video of an RSA lecture by Tim Gill (Gill 2008, online) on the subject of children's play and risk aversion. She'd felt it presented a balanced argument and asked the Deputy if they might look at some of it. But the Deputy dismissed her suggestion, saying they had a lot to cover in the meeting as it was, inferring that the 'fallout' from Florentyna's pilot study had added to her burdens. It was an uneasy meeting, with the staff member responsible for health and safety determined not to be swayed, talking about the dangers inherent in the local environment, and reminding Florentyna of what the daily morning 'sweep' of the outside area revealed. How could she guarantee the children's safety in her 'forest area'? Florentyna tried to respond that having the forest area didn't mean they would need to be less vigilant in making the children's environment safe, but there was a fine line between safety concerns and then stifling productive free play activities. Florentyna, sensing a general animosity from the rest of the staff at this point, felt she might as well give up on the whole project, when the Deputy Manager brought everyone's attention to the important changes to risk assessment procedures highlighted in the latest Early Years guidelines from the government. In it, concern had been widely expressed that too much emphasis had been placed on risk assessments, to the detriment of children's learning and development. Some members of staff were mollified by this, but others (led by the member of staff for health and safety) remained not only unconvinced but slightly antagonistic.

When Florentyna told her tutor what had happened, she was reassured that her questionnaire had been fair and balanced. 'But that isn't the real issue here, is it?', her tutor said. 'Do you remember how you felt after your literature review?'

Florentyna nodded, 'I felt staff not only "ignorant" about benefits of forest schools, but of wider issues – what it means to be a young child in this country.' As she spoke, Florentyna also acknowledged she had mentally put those thoughts in the 'too hard' box to be visited later, and had concentrated on presenting her forest school in the most positive light. Her tutor gently suggested she would need to 'resolve' the tensions in order for her research to receive a fair hearing, and asked her to consider what positive steps she might take.

After much debate with herself, Florentyna reasoned that a questionnaire for parents might help persuade staff that they were not 'in the spotlight', that she was in fact trying to gather evidence from various sources. From the anecdotal evidence she'd collected on parents' responses to the children's photographs, Florentyna felt confident the data from such a questionnaire would be positive, and, together with the positive responses she had received from the children, might perhaps help persuade staff of the real benefits of a forest school approach. After all, it was the children's health, learning and development that should be at the centre of everyone's thinking.

Florentyna, however, found designing a questionnaire for parents even more difficult than the one she'd agonised over for staff. For one thing, she couldn't rely on a common shorthand of terms, and specialist language, like 'gross and fine motor skills', 'formative assessment' or 'SEN'. From her experience, she also knew parents' knowledge and understanding of the six areas of learning within the EYFS was variable. One aspect of her practice she had always seen as positive was her ability to communicate effectively with families with English as an additional language. Did that mean she had to create two separate questionnaires, or one that was written in two languages? Given that there was a variety of languages now spoken by families accessing the setting, how could that be achieved? She needed to talk with her tutor again.

Reflection point

After much agonising, Florentyna decided that she would stick to her two original methods rather than bringing in a third. Her tutor suggested that there was some 'triangulation' going on in Florentyna's data, even if Florentyna could not yet see it clearly. He suggested that Florentyna complete her research activities and then revisit her data when she has a complete set, and in light of the literature review. It is quite common that when students are in the middle of their data collection they are unable 'to see the wood for the trees' in this way. If you are faced with a similar dilemma, do not hesitate to consult with your tutor as soon as possible.

Sunil

Sunil decided that, as lack of time now ruled out the cyclical approach of action research, he would have to go with a case study. He looked at the definition from his notes: '... *an opportunity for one aspect of a problem to be studied in some depth within a limited time scale'*. Well, he certainly had the latter.

He couldn't avoid making decisions about how to collect his data any longer. He felt most at ease observing the children while working with them at an activity. He'd developed his own shorthand over time, and had been commended by other staff for the detail in some of the observations he'd done for the children's profiles. There had been a discussion at college on something called the mosaic approach to questioning children which he really liked the sound of. He didn't feel at all confident about having to interview the reception class teacher, but he could hardly leave her out and just interview the nursery teacher; that certainly wouldn't be representative or reliable. He didn't have particularly good justifications for rejecting some of the methods he had considered, but time was really slipping by. He decided that questionnaires for the staff would be quicker and easier to deliver than doing interviews, as well as providing quantitative data that he hoped would be simpler to triangulate.

He began with what he liked doing most, working with and observing the children. The outdoor 'trains' play was a success on several levels. The boys had devised their own names for both the 'trains' and the stations they now stopped at (*know that print carries meaning and reads from left to right in English*), which he discussed with the reception teacher, after which she became rather less dismissive of his research, even asking how he was getting on one day during the following week, and showing him where she had marked up the children's profiles as a result of his activities.

At first the station names had been chalked on the playground floor, but bike tyres and young feet kept rubbing them out. Sunil discussed with the children how that might be addressed, scribing such suggestions as: *'paint it on so it won't come off', 'write it on a board in big, big letters'*. The labels for the trains hadn't fared much better; solutions ranged from: *'stick it on there'* (the front of the bike) and *'put it on his hat'* (the train driver's). Sunil helped make cardboard labels with loops of string to be worn round the train driver's neck. This became an important symbol of ownership, part of the uniform – you couldn't be a driver without a label round your neck. Not content with simply naming the stations, the boys began to construct station platforms from the hollow blocks, with seats for passengers to wait on. One of the girls from the outdoor home corner started selling 'tea' and 'coffee' at £5 a cup. Sunil asked some of the drivers how they knew where they were going, and this led to more chalk drawings of train track on the tarmac (creating some disagreement at times over which way the track should run), with Sunil writing in the station names where he was told to.

Reflecting on the descriptive narratives he'd produced during his observations, Sunil considered how he was going to turn them into usable 'data'. He recalled his tutor talking about using keyword searches for interview transcripts and wondered if that would be appropriate. He decided to put the observations to one side and concentrate on employing his 'mosaic' approach to question 'the lads'. He was in luck with the digital cameras, as part of the headmaster's new drive for creativity had resulted in the purchase of several 'jam cams' (digital cameras the children could easily use) and scanners. Sunil had become adept at using open-ended questioning, and engaging in sustained shared thinking with the children, so the mosaic approach fitted in quite naturally with his daily practice. He'd also found the reflective journal entries (which he tended to use for critical incidents only) really helped jog his memory.

The 'train journeys' had taken on a life of their own, thanks to the children's imaginative extensions. Sunil asked two of the more 'active' boys, who preferred to 'drive' the trains rather than chalk on the playground or print cardboard labels (now used for the café as well as the trains), to use a camera and recorder, taking him on a 'tour' of the trains and stations which now snaked along the perimeter of the outdoor area. Sunil soon had several young companions as he followed and listened to Devon and Amanda, who frequently raced around on the bikes with the boys, as they walked from station to station, clearly remembering the names of each, and embellishing stories of where the trains were coming from and why they were stopping at a particular station. 'This train's come from Cleethorpes – that's the seaside. I've been there with my Mum', Devon explained, as he photographed the cross-looking driver, who disagreed. 'No, I haven't – I've been to Blackpool – look, it says so on my sign.' Devon carried on regardless, 'and it's stopping here for – for petrol and a cup of tea'. He nodded in the direction of the café, 'one pound a cup.' *Five* pounds a cup, silly', said Amanda. 'Yes, that's right', replied Devon amiably, 'five pounds a cup.' Sunil realised, even if Devon was not accurately 'reading' the writing in this environment the children had created, he was showing an understanding that it stood for something important and meaningful. He doubted, however, that the reception class teacher would see it as such – what a shame as she had been increasingly positive of late! The thought reminded him that the questionnaire he had to create for staff was still on his 'to do' list.

The maps and books of photographs with captions, as well as the 'traffic light' assessments by the children of their environment, not only produced a very positive picture, but showed how engaged their emergent writing could be when linked to something they had created themselves and enjoyed. Sunil was particularly pleased with his 'team' of lads. Even Devon had wanted to write captions in the 'A Tour of our Stations' book they'd made. Sunil felt somehow this was 'real data', so much so that he actually wanted to show it to his tutor (the one person he'd been studiously avoiding for weeks). He also needed help.

As well as the two teachers, Sunil wanted to involve the TAs in his questionnaire. They had been really helpful when he'd first arrived at the setting, showing him where resources were officially kept (as well as the hidden places staff sometimes used). They had enthusiastically joined in with what they called 'Sunil's trains project'. The protocol of the staff room had also been explained, and the eldest TA, contrary to his expectations (which he now realised were a bit stereotypical), had a great way with the children and was really up-to-date in her thinking. The thought of devising a questionnaire on boys' language for such a small, mixed group of people that was appropriate and relevant almost gave Sunil a sleepless night.

Reflection point

If you were Sunil, how would you go about constructing your questionnaire? Remember now you have to balance time against quality. In a perfect world this would never happen, but in the world in which we live students do sometimes find themselves in this position. How do you think Sunil should balance one factor against the other in order to do the best job he can in the time available?

Conclusion

We leave our students in situations that are very common in the middle of a dissertation module:

Nick is concerned about the 'muddle' of his observation notes, but needs to get on with his interviews.

Ellie's methods have both 'worked', but she is worried about a lack of depth in her triangulation.

Florentyna is concerned that her triangulation has not worked effectively, and is confused by the conflicting data emanating from the different methods.

Sunil has again found time running away and needs to get a move on to get his questionnaire designed, distributed and returned before he begins eating into the time that he should be spending on his write-up.

Students often underestimate the amount of problem solving they will undertake in a dissertation module; in many ways it is rather like a 'game of life', with things never running to plan and a lack of the necessary information to engage in effective perspective-taking until it is nearly at its end! Try not to become too stressed or depressed about the mid-module 'I really don't know what I am doing here' blues, and of course, if in doubt, always consult your tutor.

Reference

Gill, T. (2008) *Risk and Childhood*: http://www.schoolsworld.tv/videos/tim-gill-risk-and-childhood?SESSaef1b61f645a7b455a8871fb2d6604e6=ba82feb40c9ea8daa85742d8b010177c [accessed 4 November 2011].

Chapter 7
Presenting your data

Stephen Newman, Pam Jarvis and Wendy Holland

Introduction

This chapter introduces some ways to present your data. You should read it in partnership with Chapter 4, which introduces you to methodology.

Triangulation

You will no doubt remember that we left Ellie and Florentyna worrying about the triangulation of their data, for very different reasons. Both were no doubt asking themselves, 'Why do I have to do this?' The notion of triangulation is not new. In surveying and mapmaking, triangulation was used to determine the relative locations of different points; the idea was that one place could be located accurately by getting a bearing on it to (or from) two other different places or objects. Thus three places were accurately located in comparison with each other - hence the term 'triangulation'. Even today, the notion of triangulation is used by satnavs to accurately fix location; however, the satnav device often uses readings from *four* satellites for an even more precise check on accuracy, illustrating that in this case the use of the prefix 'tri' does not necessarily mean 'three' in the modern usage of the word.

In research, this notion of getting an accurate 'fix' or position is reflected in the idea that, by using more than one method and getting different types of data, or by doing the research at more than one time, or in more than one place, a more accurate picture can be established, because findings from the different places, different times, or obtained using different methods, can be compared, and similarities and discrepancies explored (Bell 1999: 102-03). These different types of triangulation are sometimes termed place triangulation, data triangulation, and space triangulation (Bell 1999: 103). In fact, the use of different methods to investigate an issue is sometimes known as 'methodological triangulation' (Olsen n.d.: 3). In your work, for example, you may decide to carry out some qualitative research (interviews perhaps), investigate some quantitative data (perhaps gathered via tick-box questionnaire or quantitative observation method), and examine various policy documents (Olsen n.d.: 6). Our example students have eventually relied more heavily upon qualitative methods, but effective triangulation is still possible in this case, by comparing the themes that emerge from each set of data. You can then compare your findings gathered from these different sources and, by so doing, your findings will be more in-depth and, all things being equal, more likely to be accurate.

The nature and results of your research then have to be presented to your audience. In the case of writing a dissertation, the main audience will initially be the tutor(s) marking your work to the module outcome criteria, but you may also be using your research within your setting, possibly to inform/educate other staff in the development of practice. You will need to carefully consider the most effective ways of presenting your results.

It is crucial to remember that you are guiding your readers through your findings, not merely presenting information and expecting them to make their own sense of your findings. This is one of the mistakes that leads to the greatest amount of marks being lost from a results section, and it is not uncommonly found in the student dissertation. It is up to *you* to analyse your data properly, and inform the reader about how you made sense of your findings. An analogy can be drawn with cooking. There is a huge difference between merely putting the food on the plate in a haphazard fashion, and taking the time and trouble to present it in a way which makes it appear more attractive. As you will have seen in Chapter 3, some students will present their findings and analysis as one continuous section, while others will be presenting separate results and discussion sections. Whichever applies to you, you may well have to write the two sections simultaneously and divide them later, so that your presentation of results prepares the reader for the issues you raise in your analysis.

A crucial way of presenting your data is, of course, the use of text. However, as Miles and Huberman (1984: 79) point out, narrative text as a way of presenting data has some disadvantages. It is dispersed, sequential, often only vaguely ordered, and demands a great deal of the reader. For these reasons, diagrams, charts and tables can be a very valuable way of summarising and presenting the key aspects of your findings. They can allow you to bring together data in a carefully ordered, non-sequential way, and enable you and your eventual readers to gain insights into any patterns. Here your emerging analysis of the data, and your research focus and aims are important considerations. You have the opportunity to be inventive in how you display the data, and the way that you choose to grasp this challenge is a large element of the independence required in the dissertation/practitioner research process.

Ellie

. . . had reached the point where a visit to her tutor was due. Electronic representation of the data was something she had been avoiding, but the tables she had managed to create seemed unnecessarily long and wordy. She emailed for an appointment, but had received an 'out of office' reply. Her tutor would not be back for several days, and Ellie needed to keep the momentum going. If she stopped now, there was every possibility she might never get over this particular hurdle. She looked through her notes, knowing her tutor had talked at length about the use of ▶

e-technology and software packages, but her mind had blocked out much of what had been said, thinking she would unpick it later. It was now 'later'. A search through previous emails provided a link to a 'how to' site for analysing data using Edexcel. Nervously, Ellie began. Once started, she couldn't stop, overwhelmed by the coloured graphs, pie-charts, Venn diagrams, bar charts, and scattergraphs that were effortlessly generated by the software using her data, teasing out themes and results she hadn't yet considered. When her tutor returned, she happily presented these to her, expecting some kind of congratulation on overcoming her e-phobia. Instead, her tutor gave her a tired smile (perhaps her time away had been work, not a holiday, Ellie wondered). 'This is fine', her tutor began, but then went through each colourful display, asking Ellie to justify its inclusion. 'Do you really need two pie-charts showing the same percentages of staff engagement with the changes?' Ellie felt deflated, but by the time they had finished the session she realised ruefully that there were no easy solutions or short-cuts, and that presenting data (however colourful or pleasing to the eye) that didn't directly address her research questions, or confirm/challenge previous findings, was not clarifying but actually obscuring her key findings.

Reflection point

As Ellie has found, there is more to presenting data than creating a graph or pie-chart to describe each separate statistic. To continue the food analogy, presenting a main course by placing every item on a separate plate would not be particularly appetising. Another analogy can be drawn with music, in that we do not play every note separately, but combine them in different ways to create a melody. A key requirement in presenting data within a dissertation is that it be combined in ways that make the key findings clear to the reader; for example, 'Parents proposed that . . . but practitioners' view on the topic was . . .' or 'In observing the children it was found that . . . but the practitioner interviews suggested . . .' Look back at the previous chapter, and try to predict what types of data Ellie and Florentyna could most usefully combine to illustrate their key findings.

Tables

Tables can be a relatively straightforward way of presenting textual information in a way that can break free of the sequential or linear format that normal text follows. You can, for example, consider the responses of different individuals to various themes or questions.

	Person 1	Person 2	Person 3
Theme/Question A			
Theme/Question B			
Theme/Question C			

Here, when completed, the responses can be read 'vertically' to reveal the responses of each person across a range of themes; and 'horizontally' to reveal the different responses of each person to particular themes. In preparing this table, you will have already begun to analyse the results.

This is a relatively straightforward table. But the same format can be developed to summarise the views of different groups, as in the example below.

	Newly Qualified Teachers (NQTs)	Experienced Teachers	Senior Management
Theme A			
Theme B			
Theme C			

Tables can also be developed to present information about different themes related to, for example, different locations (Miles and Huberman 1984: 85).

Ellie draws up a table as follows:

	Practitioner Interviews	Parent Questionnaires
Theme 1: Child is 'happy'		
Theme 2: Parent has named contact		
Theme 3: Lack of flexibility		

She finds however that, due to the fact that one set of data is coming from semi-structured interviews and the other from fixed answer questionnaires, she cannot fit all her key findings on to a chart of this nature. She is still a little embarrassed about the single issue pie charts, and does not want to consult her tutor again so quickly after her previous tutorial.

Reflection point

Ellie confides in you. She says that she was embarrassed when it was pointed out to her that her charts did not present the data in any type of synthesised manner, but now she has found that she can't possibly synthesise *all* of her findings on to the chart she has created. What would you advise her to do? Remember, the key point here is to gather the data into useful sets, but not necessarily to get all of it on to just one chart!

In each case, 'the table collects data for easy viewing in one place, permits detailed analysis, and sets the stage for later . . . analysis' (Miles and Huberman 1984: 80). One example of how tabulating your results can help with later analysis is when you select specific data and put it in numerical order. Here a very useful explanation has been given by Jesson (1994), who highlights that two useful aspects can be the average (median) for your data, and a measure of how the data vary between themselves (using the inter-quartile range).

We will use the example provided by Jesson to look at these aspects in a little more detail. Suppose, for instance, that you have collected information about the teaching styles of 20 teachers. Your data in its 'raw form' might look like this:

Question asked: What percentage of the time do you use each of these teaching styles? A: 'Self-selected groups'; B: 'teacher-selected groups'; C: Class teaching.

Gender	Percentage		
	A	B	C
M	80	10	10
M	0	20	80
F	20	30	50
F	0	60	40
F	30	60	10
F	80	15	5
M	60	25	15
F	0	0	100

(Continued)

Gender	Percentage		
	A	B	C
F	80	20	0
M	60	30	10
F	20	50	30
M	10	50	40
F	30	60	10
M	40	50	10
F	90	10	0
M	60	20	20
F	50	30	20
M	40	30	30
M	25	25	50
F	20	70	10

As you can see, the data are presented in a table, but what conclusions can be drawn is none too easy to say without further work. One very simple start to the analysis could be made by stating, for each teacher, which teaching style they used the most. Thus, for example, one teacher uses Self-selected groups 90 per cent of the time, and we could tabulate the results for the group as below:

	Predominant Teaching Styles		
	Style A	Style B	Style C
Number of teachers	9	7	4

Consider: How useful is this analysis?

We might want to develop the description of the data by working out the percentage of time that the characteristic teacher of this sample uses the teaching style of 'Self-selected groups'. Here we can use the notion of the average (median). Who is the 'average' teacher in this sample of 20?

To find out, we can re-present the data for teaching style A as below:

Teaching Style A (ranked in ascending order)																			
1	2	3	4	5	6	7	8	9	10	11	12	13	14	15	16	17	18	19	20
0	0	0	10	20	20	20	25	30	30	40	40	50	60	60	60	80	80	80	90

There are 20 teachers, so the 'average' or median teacher will be the one where half the sample is above, and half the sample is below. Here the sample is an even number of 20, so there are two 'middle' positions (10 and 11), so we find the 'half-way' point by adding 1 to the sample number (20+1) and dividing by 2. Thus the median position is at 10.5. The teacher ranked number 10 uses this teaching style 30 per cent of the time, and the teacher ranked at position 11 uses this teaching style 40 per cent of the time, so the median use is halfway between these two figures (i.e. 35 per cent). This suggests that the average teacher in this sample uses teaching style A (Self-selected groups) for just over a third of the time.

This is useful information, but it does not tell us whether there is a great variation across the sample. The data presented in the table helps, and we can use that further to look at the figures for each 'quarter' or quartile.

How do we find the quartiles? As the prefix 'quart' suggests, we find the quartiles by dividing the sample size by 4. If that gives a whole number, we then add 0.5 to the result. As the sample in this example consists of 20 teachers, we divide 20 by 4 and get 5, so we add 0.5 to give us quartile divisions at positions 5.5, 10.5 and 15.5.

Teaching Style A (ranked in ascending order)																			
1	2	3	4	5	6	7	8	9	10	11	12	13	14	15	16	17	18	19	20
0	0	0	10	20	20	20	25	30	30	40	40	50	60	60	60	80	80	80	90

We can then see that the lower quartile figure for teaching style A is 20 per cent and that for the upper quartile the figure is 60 per cent, so the inter-quartile range is the difference between them (namely 40 per cent). These figures indicate how much the data vary across the sample. We could then compare it with the results for other teaching styles and see whether this style was used more or less variably.

Activity

Produce similar tables for Teaching Style B. Find the median and quartiles, and the inter-quartile range. Write a sentence which describes the results for Teaching Style B and another sentence which compares these results with those discussed above for teaching style A.

▶

Jesson's examples show that putting your results into tables is far from being just a means of presenting your results. It can also be a very important way of helping you to begin to analyse them.

Charts

Miles and Huberman (1984: 89) suggest another format that may be helpful to consider, one that they term a 'growth gradient'. Here you can see that the format is a sort of hybrid between a table and a graph. The vertical scale increases from the individual through to the national, and the horizontal scale is, in effect, a time-line.

National				
Regional				
Local				
Individual				
	2008	2009	2010	2011

Time

In this example, the completion of the boxes with appropriate information could help to show how perhaps a particular initiative had been implemented and developed. It might be that a particular initiative was first introduced at the level of an individual school (for example, to allocate pupils to self-selected groups for a minimum of 30 per cent of teaching time) but that over the course of four years it developed nationally; if so, the completion of the boxes might follow the pattern indicated by the shading, and this would give a visual aspect showing the development of the initiative, with the text providing at least a summary of some of the main aspects.

Charts can also be useful to show developments and arguments. In the example below, some key aspects of two arguments and their respective advocates (traditional and modern) are juxtaposed, and the problems clearly identified.

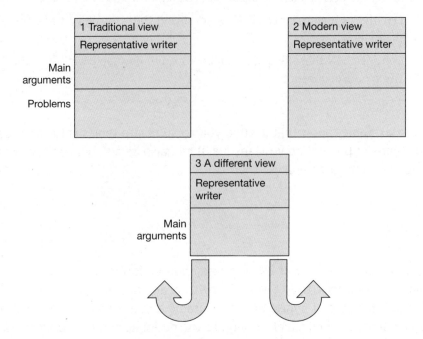

Here the format can facilitate direct comparisons between the arguments of the 'traditional' and 'modern' positions, and the clear identification of the problems of each. The implication is that the third view offers a way of resolving these problems, and that it can be used in some way to resolve (or dissolve) the issues identified with arguments 1 and 2. Note that this diagram presents a useful format for displaying the structure of your analysis which will follow, but the diagram itself is a reflection of your emerging analysis of the data/information that you have researched.

Activity

Reproduce the chart above and replace the terms 'traditional' and 'modern' with 'Scandinavian' and 'Anglo-American'. Consider how Florentyna might make use of a chart of this type to make sense of the literature she has reviewed, and subsequently use this chart to consider deeper explanations of the dichotomy between the observation and questionnaire data with which she has been wrestling.

▶

Reflection point

It is worth noting at this point that such a diagram may usefully help you to understand the complexities of particular arguments, and the key points of similarity and difference between them. That being so, you may find devising such a diagram useful; even if like Florentyna you are not intending to use it in this format in your final write-up, you may find it a very valuable means of ensuring that you structure your narrative arguments clearly.

Another idea that might be useful is the 'sociogram', which can be used to show some of the relationships in a class. You may have used this before in routine child observations; it is quite a common method used when investigating complaints of 'bullying', or a child being 'excluded' by others in a group. Hopkins (1985: 139–40) describes how such a diagram can be used and some potential associated issues worth considering. A crucial point here is that the sociogram describes the situation clearly, in a way that would be very difficult and complicated to do using text.

Example sociogram

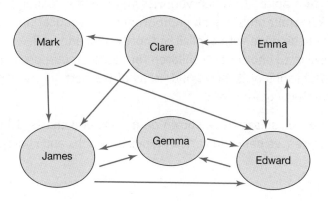

One issue that is worth considering is whether such a chart or diagram may oversimplify a complex situation. Tables, for example, usually demand that information be placed in a specific 'box', and that differences be highlighted and emphasised. In reality, a situation is likely to be far more complex. One way of dealing with this in charts is to use the same notion as is used in Venn diagrams, with overlapping areas of two or more circles representing the things in common, and the separate sections highlighting the key differences.

Imagine completing this diagram for the staff in your setting, for example:

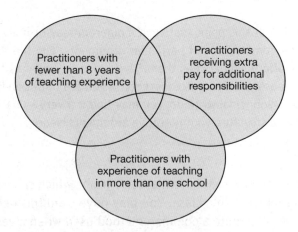

Here you can see that the diagram can represent some of the complexities of a specific situation more clearly than a long narrative.

Another approach that you might like to consider if it 'fits' within your research topic is the use of maps and photographs to represent data or other important information. If, for example, your research involves some discussion of classroom layout, it may be hard for the reader to develop an understanding from a purely written description. A map or a photograph is likely to be far more useful. Important points to which you wish to draw the reader's attention can be labelled. Remember that taking photographs in an educational context must always and only be done with explicit authorisation, and while you are unlikely to get permission to photograph children for research purposes in Early Years settings, photographs of displays and areas of the setting are usually permissible and potentially quite useful.

Some data are well suited to be shown on graphs and charts. There are some important differences between various types of graphs and charts.

A line graph

These are used when the data being shown are 'continuous'. For example, if we plot children's temperatures, we would use a line graph, because temperature change is continuous, even if it can sometimes be rapid. A line graph which plots air temperatures would require a vertical axis that extends downwards to show minus numbers; however, for the type of research that you will carry out it is most likely that the vertical axis will start at zero. Note however that it should not start at a number higher than zero, but you can then choose the 'steps' from this point to display your data as clearly as possible, e.g. 1, 2, 3/2, 4, 6/5, 10, 15 . . . etc.

A bar chart

A bar chart is used when the data are 'discontinuous'. For example, rainfall is shown using a bar chart, because when rain falls needs to be recorded with respect to a particular day, week, month etc. We are readily able to decide, should we need to, which day, or which week, or month, or year, any particular rain fell. The height of each bar represents the amount. The divisions should start at 0 and work upwards in evenly spaced intervals as described above. Each bar should be the same width, and separated from the others by a small gap. The small gap between each bar represents the discontinuous nature of the data.

Sunil

. . . decides to use a bar chart to represent the number of children engaging in his literacy activities over the period of a fortnight, using separate bars for boys and for girls. He reflects that it would have been a good idea to do this at the beginning of his research, as he is fairly sure that more and more children took part over the first few days, but he realises that this chance has now disappeared. He has read that, to be eligible for all the marks available, he has to present some of his data on charts and graphs, and he remembers drawing bar charts in primary school, so surely this is the least stress option.

Reflection point

Do *you* think that Sunil has picked the 'least stress option'? What data do you think you would chart, and how, if you were carrying out research on the same topic?

A histogram

A histogram looks very similar to a bar chart, but it is the area of the bars (rather than their height) which is important. Suppose you have collected some data about the age distribution of children in a particular setting (Columns A and B below).

A Age of children (in years)	B Number (Frequency)	C Relative frequency
0-2	14	7
2-3	12	12
3-4	10	10
4-5	11	11

Here, if we draw a bar chart, a problem would occur because the division for the age of the children varies. The 0-2 age range is twice that for the other groupings. So before we can plot these figures on a histogram, we need to halve the frequency for the 0-2 range. This will give us the 'relative frequency' (Column C), which we can then plot on to a histogram.

Histogram to show age distribution of children

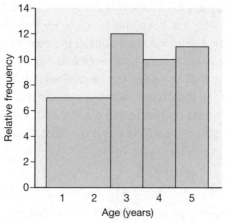

A scattergraph

A scattergraph is used to help to show the relationship between two factors, usually called 'variables'. Suppose, for example, that we wish to compare children's age and height. Our starting point would probably be that children's height (in general) depends on their age, in which case we would call 'height' the dependent variable, and their age the independent variable.

We would then draw a graph like this:

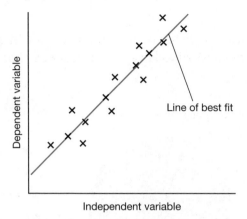

Source: http://www.mathsrevision.net/gcse/pages.php?page=10

We would then plot (with an X on the example above) each child's age and height, using both axes. Having done so, we will have a number (15 in this example) of Xs marked. Statistical applications are readily able to then draw the 'best-fit line', but these can be approximated by hand-drawing a line which has the same number of Xs above and below it (6 in each case in this example). We can see that most Xs are fairly close to this line, and that the line goes upwards from left to right. The first tells us that there is a strong (although not total) positive correlation between a child's age and height, and the second that the height of older children tends to be more than of younger children, but that this is not invariably so.

Reflection point/Activity

Nick decides to draw a scattergram that maps children's calendar age against their level of numeracy competence from their EYFS profiles. What type of correlation do you think he will get? Do you think it stands to be strong or weak? You could try this out with the children in your setting. You do not have to use numeracy as your focus; for example, if you work with younger children you could look at various physical competencies, or language development.

Pie-charts

These are used to show the percentage breakdown of one set of data. They are familiar to most people and, at their best, offer a very clear representation of the data. To draw one, the raw figures you have in your research need to be converted to percentages. Technically this is not difficult and most standard word processing/data processing software can produce pie charts very quickly – as Ellie discovered!

One key decision is therefore that of deciding which format of the many offered is most suitable. Some easily available figures were used below to produce the following pie-charts.

Pie-charts to show estimated groupings of UK population in 1999

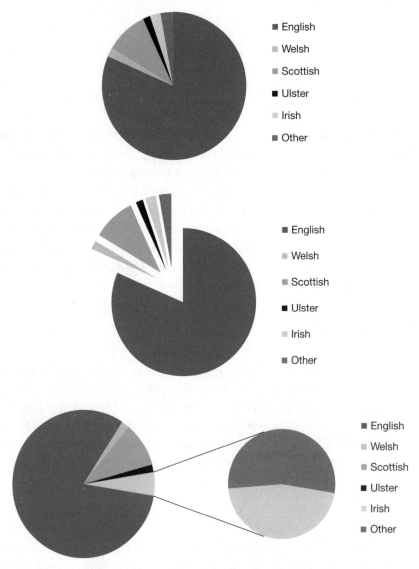

Data source: http://www.bmf.org.uk/media/learninglibrary//Key%20- Skills%20-%20 Application%20Of%20Number/Pie%20Charts%20Part%202.pdf

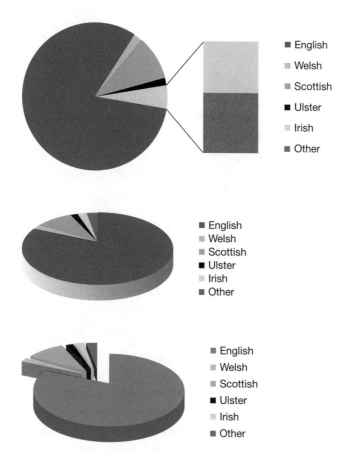

Activity

Collect data relating to the age of children in your setting and record their calendar month of birth. Run the data in the pie-chart formats that are available to you on your computer and then consider which format you think is best, and why, and in what other ways these data might have been shown. How important are chart colours and any 3D effects? What are some of the disadvantages of pie-charts?

Reflection point 1

Do you think if Ellie had gone through this exercise before presenting her tutor with her vast range of pie-charts she might have considered how to organise the data at rather more length before 'pushing the button'?

▶

Reflection point 2

In charting his class's birth months, Nick has found that 62 per cent of his children were born between April and August, while one of his dissertation group mates finds out when carrying out the same exercise that 70 per cent of her children were born between September and March. How might this information be of use to a school classroom-based practitioner?

Note that pie-charts are not in themselves an analysis of the data; they merely present it. In addition, by themselves, they do not make clear the size of the data set. A pie-chart which is based on a sample of, say, 10 people will in general look the same as one based on a sample of several hundred. That may give spurious legitimacy to a very small sample – something to remember when you come to discuss reliability, validity and generalisability (see Chapter 8).

Leading on from the example above, a further consideration is that, as you are developing your diagrams, charts and tables, it is likely (even desirable) that your thoughts will evolve as you move through your data analysis. This being so, it is important not to become too dogmatic in the early stages of developing ways of presenting your data; be prepared to think creatively, and to change your ideas as you proceed; 'to scout around, sleuth, and take second and third looks' at the data (Miles and Huberman 1984: 89). Of course, this willingness to adapt and to try new ideas makes demands on your time but this investment is an essential part of finding the best ways of showing the data and itself becomes part of the analytical process. As has been previously mentioned, 'experimenting' with different ways of showing your data may help you to discover previously unthought-of lines of enquiry. So be prepared to try different ideas, but remember that not all of them may be worth including in your final piece of work.

Common pitfalls when creating charts and diagrams

As mentioned previously, diagrams, charts and tables can be useful ways of presenting information in a clear way. However, there are common pitfalls that you should try to avoid.

The first type of pitfall is the 'unnecessary' diagram, chart or table. Consider the example below.

Example 1: The unnecessary

Participants in the survey

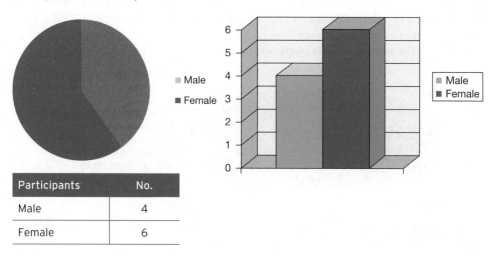

Participants	No.
Male	4
Female	6

Suppose you have interviewed ten people, of whom four were male and six were female. Is a bar chart such as the one above showing this information helpful? Does the '3D' aspect of the bar chart help? Does it add anything to aid clarity that a sentence stating the numbers cannot achieve? It is fairly obvious that the pie-chart and the table show the same information, but we are providing you with this example because we have all marked dissertations where the sample information has been presented in this way, on both pie-chart and block graph! Again, with the small numbers involved it is arguable that neither adds much to clarity. Consider whether the proportion of males and females interviewed is relevant for your study. If not, why mention the issue at all?

Another aspect of the issue of unnecessary diagrams is where the same information is shown in different ways. Again, considering the example above, even if you decide that it is important to represent in graphical form the number of male and female participants, it is unlikely to be appropriate to have a table, a bar graph and a pie-chart.

Example 2: The over-complicated

The second example moves us from the 'unnecessary' to the 'overcomplicated'. In the example below is a pie-chart. Notice that it has been presented from an oblique angle and this, you may consider, is not especially helpful. However, when you examine the pie-chart carefully, you may be wondering what it shows. It is by no means clear what the booking is a percentage of; if we interpret the key we might be led to think that the room is booked for 71 per cent of the available time, but this is not stated. If this is the case, do we need the pie-chart? It seems unnecessary. If we do, do we need the key which has eleven labels, only two of which are used? This is a typical example of the overcomplicated.

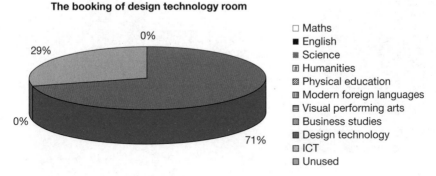

Example 3: The over-crowded

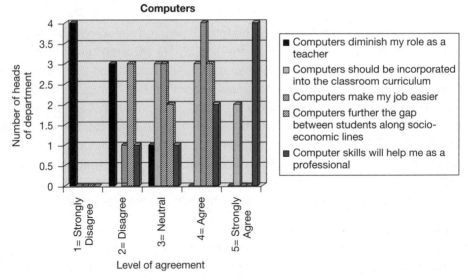

Just as a pie-chart with more than about five divisions becomes unwieldy, a graph with many thin columns can become impossible to read. Legends or keys with numerous so-called explanations can confuse rather than clarify.

Reflection point

What issues arise from the above graph? Can you think of alternative methods that could have been used to show this information?

Example 4: The 'all my findings are here' approach

Attitudes towards Computer Use questionnaire - Result

Attitudes towards Computer Use	1 = Strongly Disagree	2 = Disagree	3 = Neutral	4 = Agree	5 = Strongly Agree
I would like every student in my classes to have access to a computer	0	0	1	1	6
Computer skills are essential to students	0	0	0	2	6
I feel tense when people start talking about computers	2	3	3	0	0
I feel pressure from others to integrate the computer more into my classroom	0	5	3	0	0
I would like my students to be able to use the computer more	0	0	1	4	3
Computers are dehumanising	2	2	4	0	0
I avoid the computer whenever possible	5	3	0	0	0
Computer instruction is just another fad	5	3	0	0	0
The use of computers should be confined to computer courses	5	3	0	0	0
I like using the computer to solve complex problems	0	1	3	4	0
More training would increase my use of the computer in the classroom	0	0	1	6	1
Computers diminish my role as a teacher	4	3	1	0	0
Computers should be incorporated into the classroom curriculum	0	0	3	3	2
Computers make my job easier	0	1	3	4	0
Computers further the gap between students along socio-economic lines	0	3	2	3	0
Computer skills will help me as a professional	0	1	1	2	4
Learning computers makes high demands on my professional time	0	3	3	2	0
Computers change my role as a teacher	1	1	3	3	0
I can help others solve computer problems	1	2	2	3	0
Computers enhance classroom instruction	0	1	1	5	1

Example 5: The 'needs more explanation' chart

Family Responsibilities and Management Role

	Women	Men
Numbers of managers citing family responsibilities as impeding their ability to perform their management role	10	3
Numbers of managers *not* citing family responsibilities as impeding their ability to perform their management role	4	11

Reflection point

Can you think of more effective ways of displaying the data contained in Examples 4 and 5?

Conclusion

As you have now discovered, the act of charting or tabulating data needs a lot of thought and, in this age of the easy production of a very professional looking chart, table or graph by simply pressing a button, not a little restraint! In all cases, remember that the inclusion of a chart or graph should only be undertaken if you are sure that it will aid your reader in understanding your analysis of the data. *Never* include a chart or graph 'because you have to' or 'because it will make it look like I know what I am doing'. Charts or graphs that are included for the latter reason inevitably tend to have the opposite effect. Consider thoroughly what charts/graphs you plan to include while you are carrying out the initial analyses of your data, and make sure that you budget some of your tutorial time to discuss these with your tutor before making a final decision. This is most definitely a key aspect where 'proper preparation prevents poor performance'.

References

Barcelona Field Studies Centre S.L. (2011) Data Presentation: Pie Charts, online: http://geographyfieldwork.com/DataPresentationPieCharts.htm.

Bell, J. (1999) *Doing your research project: a guide for first-time researchers in education and social science*, 3rd edition, Maidenhead: Open University Press.

Builders Merchants Federation (2011) Key Skills: Pie charts, online: http://www.bmf.org.
uk/media/learninglibrary//Key%20Skills%20-%20Application%20Of%20Number/
Pie%20Charts%20Part%202.pdf.

Coles, A. and McGrath, J. (2010) *Your Education Research Project Handbook*, Harlow:
Pearson Education.

Hopkins, D. (1985) *A Teacher's Guide to Classroom Research*, 2nd edition, Buckingham:
Open University Press.

Jesson, D. (1994) *What are the quantitative aspects of your research?*, Sheffield:
University of Sheffield Division of Education.

MathsRevision (2011) Representing data, online: http://www.mathsrevision.net/gcse/
pages.php?page=10.

Miles, M.B. and Huberman, A.M. (1984) *Qualitative Data Analysis: A Sourcebook of New
Methods*, London: Sage Publications.

Olsen, W. (n.d.) Triangulation in Social Research: Qualitative and Quantitative Methods
Can Really Be Mixed, online: http://www.ccsr.ac.uk/staff/Triangulation.pdf.

Chapter 8
Discussing and concluding: placing your findings within the frame of Early Years research

Pam Jarvis and Wendy Holland

Introduction

As we have stated in Chapter 3, the results and discussion can be presented in the same or in separate sections of your dissertation. In general, qualitative research will be presented in a combined findings and analysis section, and quantitative research in separate results/discussion sections. There are various compromises for research using both qualitative and quantitative methods. A final decision on how to present these sections should be made in consultation with your tutor.

Whichever type of write-up you are undertaking, it is still crucial that you do the following:

● Write critically and analytically

● Revisit the literature

● Revisit reliability/validity/representativeness

● Reflect in ways that usefully inform practice in Early Years, including development of your own practice, and development of practice within the setting.

Students writing dissertations frequently find this the most challenging aspect of their process, but if you are organised it does not need to be. One of the biggest problems is running out of time at the point at which you begin the discussion/conclusion of your studies, and you should make all efforts to avoid this.

Sunil's

. . . dissertation tutor sought him out on one of his college days to ask whether he had begun to consider his discussion/conclusion. Sunil explained to her the progress that his lads had made, and that even the reception teacher was now coming on board to some extent, having seen the positive impact that his activities had made on some of the children's EYFS profiles. 'That is great, Sunil', she replied. 'I remember at the last tutorial thinking that your study was an excellent example of how a student dissertation can actually move practice on in a setting, and have a really positive effect. You clearly have a lot to say about how your research has moved practice on in the setting, and developed your own understanding of the potential breadth of literacy and pre-literacy activities. However . . . what are you going to say with respect to how your results tie into the literature? Also, how reliable and valid do you think your methodology was? Don't leave this so late that you don't get the marks that you could have had for properly exploring these aspects. You need some time to revisit your literature review and really think about these points. You should be making notes on them now.' Sunil made a mental note to spend some time in the library that lunchtime, reading through his literature review, which he has not revisited for some time.

▶

Reflection point

As Sunil is beginning to discover, the marks for effectively relating findings to the literature review, and for deep methodological reflection, are the ones that are most commonly lost in the undergraduate dissertation. The sad thing is that, generally, this happens not because students are not capable of doing it, but because they run out of time. Reflective thought needs a calm mind, and it is very difficult to achieve this when you seem to have a big clock ticking inside your head. As you come to the end of your data analysis, what time have you put aside to calmly contemplate what your data actually means in the research, rather than in the practitioner sense? If, like Sunil, you find this difficult to do at home or at work, what opportunity do you have during your college days to get some quiet time in the library? Make sure you schedule this into your study plans over at least the last six weeks of your dissertation module, and, preferably, over the final two months. Start now, by making some notes in your journal about how you will manage the 'discussion' aspect of your report.

Writing critically and analytically

The first point to make here, following on from the section above, is that critical and analytical thought does not occur quickly, or when the person trying to be critical and analytical is under pressure to do so. During the period in which you are carrying out your analysis, you should make sure that you are never very far away from paper and pen so you can note random thoughts that occur to you about your research, to revisit in your study periods. Guy Claxton proposes that in our over-busy lives we let what he dubs the 'hare brain' take control of our thoughts, where in fact it is the slower 'tortoise mind' in which the 'intelligent unconscious' is located (Claxton 1997). When you are analysing research results, you need both of these modes of thought – the deep slow contemplation, and the more 'surface' organisational thinking. Making notes when thoughts occur to you, and then organising these during designated study times nearly always makes for a more thorough analysis.

Nick

. . . sits eating a sandwich at his desk one lunchtime. He contemplates that it is a relief to have decided (in agreement with his tutor) that his data collection phase is now at an end. He reflects that, after a somewhat rocky start,

▶

his relationship with the TAs now seems much improved, and that his dissertation process has largely been responsible for this. The TAs certainly approved of the changes in the role play area he'd introduced, one of them being overheard saying after her interview that she now felt 'part of the research "team"', rather than one of its subjects! Nick realised on reflection that his first attempts at gathering data had not been quite ethical. He'd almost tried to press-gang the TAs into completing questionnaires that showed their mathematical competence (or incompetence, he now realised) and had clearly shown his frustration at their non-compliance. He cringed on reflection about how he would feel if someone asked him to complete a questionnaire relating to his evaluation of his skills in actively engaging with the children's role play. How awkward the TAs must have felt, when he'd demanded to know why they'd not completed his carefully worded questionnaires! He realised now he'd been nervous at the time about doing the research and too focused on *his own* needs.

Reflection point

How can Nick translate this train of thought into a discursive analysis of his own methods? When he considers this himself, sitting quietly with his laptop in his little 'office' at home, he finds himself revisiting the ethics guidelines. Have a look at your ethics guidelines and see if you can then write some analytical bullet points about Nick's initial plans for his method.

Revisiting the literature

The first point to make here is that literature reviews should not be set in stone until the discussion is written. What often happens is that your own research opens up a range of new reflections about the topic, and you may then be able to root within an area of the literature that you did not previously think 'fitted' in the literature review. On the other hand, you may find that a piece of literature you initially thought was pivotal did not really turn out to be particularly helpful. It is always open to you to re-write to reflect this situation. The problem that then sometimes arises is a lack of thorough recording of sources read within the literature review process . . . but, hopefully, you will have followed the 'keep record sheets' advice in Chapter 3, so this will not apply to you!

Ellie

. . . has indeed kept meticulous record sheets when undertaking her literature review, but her confusion over her results has rather sapped her confidence when it comes to 'making sense' of her data. The main aspect that she fears is that she has raised an insolvable problem, in that it now seems very clear to her that the key person cannot adequately substitute for a parent. She finds herself getting very close to tears when she thinks about taking this news back to the management of her setting, and discusses her fears with her tutor. Her tutor asks her whether the fundamental question about caring for children at home or in daycare was part of her original research question. Ellie thinks about this for a moment and says, 'No, I wanted to improve the way that we organise key person allocation and practice by . . .' (looking at her notes) '. . . considering *to what extent* a key person could address a child's need for a bonded relationship.' 'And what information have you got on this?', asks her tutor. Ellie contemplates for a moment and says, 'Ah, I see . . . I have got quite a lot, haven't I?' She then begins to consider a lecture in second-year child development about the effect of cortisol on stress reactions in small children, and the positive effect of well-run settings. 'So', she continues, 'what I have done is gather some ideas about how we can do the very best we can to provide a calm, secure and caring environment for the children, in a society in which many parents simply do not have the choice to care for them at home.' She rifles through her folder and finds the record sheet relating to an article she sourced on this in the early stage of her literature review, when she systematically went through all the material on attachment that she had covered in years one and two of the course. Her tutor smiles at her.

Reflection point

Could you find a source as easily as this? If not, it is worth spending a study session or two to organise your literature review notes prior to making a start on writing the discussion aspect of your report (whether this is a separate section, or analytical comments within a findings section). Having to break off to really 'dig' for a source when you have got into a deeply analytical train of thought usually has a significant 'derailing' effect.

Revisiting reliability/validity/representativeness

Students often spend a lot of 'empty' time fretting about the reliability, validity and representativeness of a study that has been undertaken within one Early Years setting. They are typically taught that meeting the criteria for a reliable, valid and representative research study is a large sample of participants studied within a range of environments. Where this is applied to professional research this is a powerful argument, but when it is applied to a student dissertation it can unnecessarily sap a student's confidence and lead to a lot of unfounded stress. The undergraduate or master's dissertation/practitioner research assignment is not designed to break new ground in the relevant academic field, but to allow the student to learn about research methods, to develop their own practice knowledge and, if it is undertaken within a professional setting, to positively impact upon the practice in that setting. In this sense, if the student has undertaken the methodology in an informed and careful fashion (see Chapter 4), they do not need to agonise over the smallness of their sample and the narrowness of the research environment. All they need to do is to consider in their analysis how reliable/valid/representative their results can be claimed to be within their own practice and within their practice environment; for example, Nick's and Ellie's considerations above put them on the road to useful evaluations of this nature. The other point that needs to be made in your write-up – just once – is to recognise the limitations of these findings and explain that a more extensive study would need to be undertaken before the results could be applied to practice within other settings. Within Early Years in particular, it can also help to consider how your findings might apply (or not) within a different type of professional environment (for example, in a classroom if you are in a daycare environment, or vice versa).

Reflection point

What differences might Ellie find in a classroom setting with regard to 'key people'? Consider here with careful reference to the age range one would find in a classroom catering to children within the EYFS, as opposed to the age range one would find within a daycare setting (where Ellie is located).

Reflecting in ways that usefully inform practice in Early Years, including development of researcher's own practice, and development practice within the setting

As this section is about reflection, it is logical that we should begin with a reflection point.

Reflection point

So far, you have caught up with Sunil, Nick and Ellie. Looking back over the previous chapters, can you write a paragraph for each of them under the following headings:

This dissertation has the potential to inform (name of student)'s practice in the following ways:

and

This dissertation has the potential to inform the practice in (name of student)'s setting in the following ways:

It is often easier to do this type of exercise with someone else's dissertation, because you have the benefit of 'looking in from the outside'. This task should help you gain a little perspective, from which point you may find it less difficult to carry out the same type of reflection on your own dissertation. You can also get extra practice by doing this type of exercise in small groups with your own dissertation module colleagues at college.

Hopefully, having carried out this reflection, you will see that very few people get to the end of a dissertation process without being able to offer *some* thoughts relating to the development of their own/their setting's practice, even if this largely equates to how *not* to do something! Our example students can all say something very positive about the impact of their dissertations on the development of their own and their settings' practice, and we find this applies to the vast majority of the students that we support. However, if for whatever reason you have found that ideas you have trialled in your research process really have not worked, you can still get an excellent grade for your assignment (yes, really)! Research is just that - research. Sometimes ideas work, and sometimes they don't. The key to a good grade for the assignment is to accept your data, and then to *explain* it. If you have piloted a set of ideas that have not worked, what you need to do (with the help of your tutor) is to consider why this might be so, by undertaking a thorough evaluation of your methodology and the literature that you have cited.

In our experience, some of the best grades that we have awarded have been to students who have undertaken a thorough, objective evaluation of their own methodology, finally spelling out in their conclusions what they would change if they were able to carry out the project again. On the other hand, some of the lowest marks we have awarded have been to students whose methodology clearly didn't work, and who used the words allowed for the discussion and analysis to try to argue that their review of the literature and methodology were flawless! Whatever the mixture of data and literature you have to underpin your discussion, your aim should be to analyse and evaluate your study clearly, logically and thoughtfully. If you take this as a starting point, and consult your tutor to discuss points of confusion, whatever has occurred up to this stage of the dissertation, as long as you have carried out all the processes required, you should be able to move forward to a positive result.

Florentyna

. . . worriedly re-reads her dissertation module handbook. She has now finished analysing her results, and realises that, as she feared, the two methods that she used are not telling her the same thing at all. In simple summary, where her observations have indicated that the children have engaged in deep learning through play activity in her 'forest school' area, the practitioners' attitudes towards her development of practice have been lukewarm at best. She turns to her reflective analysis, which has the effect of making her wondering whether she was wrong all along. When she started her practitioner research module, she had thought that reading in three-and-a-half languages was such a benefit; now she reflects that muddling so many cultures together in her mind might have actually been detrimental. Would a practitioner who had grown up in England, and who had more prior experience in childcare and education have come into the research with a greater understanding of the potential for resistance to outdoor free play activity among a group of practitioners in an Early Years setting before they started? Would this have then meant that they started from a different point, and would have been able to make more sense of the whole milieu, and at an earlier point in the process? After a sleepless night, she makes an appointment for a tutorial. Her tutor listens to her worries sympathetically, and then draws her attention to a comparison they have been making this semester in the 'Education in the Early Years' module between practice in Scandinavian countries and England. Florentyna thinks for a moment, and then says, 'Do you mean the research that shows, although children in Scandinavian countries begin formal education much later than children in England, the Scandinavian children seem to have better developed academic skills in their mid-teens than young people in England?' Her tutor nods. 'And many will have attended real forest schools where the practice I developed just in one small area will be the ethos of the whole setting . . .', Florentyna continues.

Florentyna's tutor suggests that she go back to her interview data to consider potential reasons for the staff's lack of enthusiasm for the practice in Florentyna's forest school area. When she considers her themes more deeply, she realises that most of those she has identified relate to adults commenting on their *own* experiences rather than those of the children ('hate getting cold and wet'/'worry if I can't see all of the children all of the time'). Where they do relate to the children's experiences, more positive themes emerged ('seemed to focus for a longer time'/'played together without fighting'). Florentyna pulls out her very dog-eared Early Years Foundation Stage guide. She remembers a thought she had about a possible comparison with the highly child-centred New Zealand Ti Whaariki guidelines during the 'Education in Early Years' module last week.

Reflection point

Florentyna is finding out that, just because the data she has collected in one method does not necessarily directly correlate with data that she has collected using another, this does not mean that she cannot comment on triangulation in her discussion. In fact, what she has is probably *more* interesting than two sets of data which exactly correspond – it has the potential to lead her to a more deeply discursive and analytical paragraph on this point. Also, she reflects, she can really deeply consider her own cultural background with reference to that of the setting in her reflective analysis. Not only is not all lost, but looking at her data in this light it would seem to have a lot of potential within the right analytical frame.

It is very common to find discrepancies between observational and interview data in this fashion. While the differences Florentyna has found are maybe more extreme than average, it is unlikely that other practitioners will perceive

▶

exactly what you perceive, particularly if they have limited experience and their qualifications are at a pre-degree level. It is very common with respect to the Early Years dissertation that the researcher has a more extensive knowledge of theoretical child development than their interview participants. This does not mean that their observations and reflections are not valuable – in fact, they can frequently be a pivotal factor in developing a wider/deeper perspective on your research topic – but where you are working in a similar situation to Florentyna in particular, the best approach to take is *caveat emptor* (literally, buyer beware!).

What *not* to do in a research report discussion: a summary

- Do not introduce literature for the first time – focus on relating your findings to the content of the literature review. This is why the final draft of the literature review is not usually produced before the end of the research and write-up process.

- Do not try to gloss over faults in the methodology – no-one's method is perfect, and the discussion is the place to highlight faults and discuss how they might be avoided in future research.

- Do not engage the reader in excessive/inappropriate reflections on the idiosyncrasies of your participants. Undergraduate students need to demonstrate that they understand that small sample research has poor generalisability, but once this is established they need to 'move on'. If you are taking a practitioner research module, it will be expected that you will explore the usefulness of your findings for your own practice within a specific setting. Some dissertation modules will also require this approach, while others will want you to take a more theoretical/empirical literature-focused approach. If in doubt, consult your module handbook and your tutor.

- Do not indicate that you have a weak/poor focus on your research question(s) by creating a vague, 'rambling' text. A good tip here is that those grading your project are not expected to work out for themselves what the relevance of your findings are within the scope of the literature and within the area of your own practice. The learning outcomes for your module, whether dissertation or practitioner research, will no doubt require that you demonstrate your understanding of these factors, and, as such, if you do not make these points clear in your write-up, the result will be a very low grade. If you find that you are struggling in this respect, do refer to your tutor for help.

Remember that they have supervised many projects and therefore will be unlikely to view putting you back on to the required 'road' as the impossible prospect that you are probably thinking it will be!

Conclusions

It is typical for students to worry about conclusions all the way through a write-up, but by the time they get there they find that this section more or less writes itself. At this point, you should be able to reiterate what you have deduced that your research actually 'told' you about your practice and that of the setting, and what improvements could be made *in your setting* in the area of practice that you researched. From this point, some reflective comments about 'what you know now' as opposed to what you 'knew then' tend to arise naturally. You may have to spend a little more time in the 'tortoise mind' phase for dissertation modules requiring a separate 'reflective analysis' section, however.

Nick has to do a 500-word reflective analysis at the end of his dissertation, considering what he has learned about himself as a teacher and his orientation to practice. You should know him quite well by this stage of the book, so why not have a go at planning this for him, in short bullet point notes if you do not have a lot of time to allocate to this activity? Once you have done this, you should feel a little more confident to do your own reflective analysis (if this is required in your dissertation). Again, as outlined above, you can get more practice at this if you get together with other students in small groups of three and four to discuss.

And finally: words and phrases to avoid in research reports

There are some words and phrases that are like 'a red rag to a bull' when tutors come across them while grading dissertations. The following list considers some of the most typical examples:

- *Bad, good, nice, terrible, stupid* and *true, perfect, an ideal solution*: avoid all subjective judgements of this nature

- *I was surprised to learn* . . . : might beg the comment, 'Why, didn't you investigate the topic thoroughly enough, then?'

- *In terms of*: vague, and a word limit-wasting phrase

- *Lots of/number of*: *how* many?

- *Kind of/type of/something like/just about/probably*: hedging your bets?

- *Obviously, clearly*: be careful: is it really obvious/clear to *everyone*?

- *Simple*: again, really? To whom?

- *You will read about* . . . : never address the reader as 'you' in an academic text

- *We will discover*: *and* never intimate that your reader is somehow your 'partner in research'. This is even more irritating than 'you' in some ways to English readers in particular, who cannot help thinking of Queen Victoria's much lampooned 'Royal We'!

- *I will describe* . . . : when at all possible, try to use the third person/passive voice: 'x will be described. . . .' (see Chapter 3)

- *Hopefully*: can sound a bit desperate

- *. . . a famous researcher* . . . : who? A reference should be provided

- *Must/always/should*: really? who says so?

- *Proof and prove*: Very little is ever proven within the social sciences; research findings merely *support* or *challenge* previous empirical findings and accepted theories. This is particularly the case for small-scale research carried out by individual student researchers

- *The can/may confusion*: in the words of my Key Stage 3 English teacher, when asked 'can I go to the toilet', you probably *can*, but you definitely *may* not!

So, your dissertation is now nearly complete, and the hand-in date is presumably looming. But do try to find the time to consider the points in our final chapter, which follows, to help you to put that extra 'polish' on to your final draft, aiming for the maximum possible marks.

Reference

Claxton, G. (1997) *Hare Brain, Tortoise Mind*, London: Fourth Estate.

Chapter 9
Presentation of report: gaining marks for 'readability'

Stephen Newman and Pam Jarvis

Introduction

Your dissertation is where you present your work in its final coherent form. It is therefore important that it represents your very best standard of work in every respect. While it may seem obvious, do make sure you leave sufficient time for draft-reading and spelling/grammar checks. Lack of time to carry out such checks is a very common reason for marks being unnecessarily lost by dissertation students, which is a great shame when it is considered how much time has been spent on the project up to this point.

Finalising the title

Many people imagine that finalising the title is something that needs to be done before even beginning their dissertation or piece of research. In fact, it is likely that you will only come to finalise your title at the end of your work. This is because your work will probably have evolved as you produced it, and you may well have written a piece of work that has a different emphasis from that which you originally envisaged in your dissertation proposal.

Florentyna

. . . is wrestling with two issues: first whether she should mention the differences between the two types of data that she collected in her title (as it seems a defining quality of the project to her), and then, if she does so, how to say this as subtly and tactfully as possible in English. Where she would know how to do this in her first language, and her English is very competent in the everyday sense, she sometimes struggles to find more subtle phraseology. She discusses her problem with the college librarian, who directs her to a thesaurus. In the end she decides on the uncontroversial 'Trialling a forest school area in an English Children's Centre'.

Reflection point

Looking back at Florentyna's progress in the previous chapters, what would you have chosen as a title? Don't forget the ethical requirement to show your final write-up to all who have participated in your research.

When finalising your title, there are several factors that you may wish to take into account. First is the importance of including specialist terms that may help to orient others to your work. For example, it seems probable that, for a piece of work investigating some aspect of Early Years, the term Early Years - or similar - should be included somewhere. See for example Florentyna's identification of her setting as a 'Children's Centre'; examples of other terms that will immediately locate your research in Early Years are 'nursery', 'daycare' or 'pre-school'.

A second consideration is to keep your title reasonably short, but to make it informative. It needs to give the potential reader a clear indication of the scope of your work and the main lines of enquiry. One way of doing this is to think of a main title, and then to have a subsidiary phrase after a colon which gives more detail, for example:

- *Closing the gender gap: problems faced by nursery and reception teachers*

- *Models of effective leadership in Early Years settings: a critical examination*

- *Teacher stress and burnout: coping strategies for teacher well-being*

Titles phrased in the form of a question do not read well, and should be avoided.

Activity

Think of a range of titles for Nick, Ellie and Sunil's projects. If you are reading this book in company with other students in your dissertation module, why not all come up with a title for each of the projects and then compare notes? You will probably be surprised at the range of variation.

Writing an abstract

The abstract is usually written in the third person, and is placed at the beginning of the work to give the potential reader a summary of the issue that was investigated, the main approaches used, and the general conclusions reached. It is conventional practice to preface all social science research reports with an abstract; this practice developed so that those searching for published research on a specific topic could browse a list of abstracts to ascertain more quickly which reports would be most likely to offer relevant information. The length of the abstract will vary according to circumstances, but about 200 to 300 words would be the usual length for the abstract for a dissertation of 6000 to 10,000 words.

Activity

Again, in company with other students in your dissertation group if possible, think up a set of bullet points covering the information that our example students should each include in their abstract. Get together and compare notes, followed by each person in the group working independently to construct one of the abstracts, then get together and compare notes again. Remember the old psychologists' maxim: an abstract should leave the reader knowing: what was done, why it was done, who the participants were, what was found.

▶

> ## Reflection point
>
> Abstract writing is another of those skills that improves with practice. You will find that the abstract you write for your own project will be much improved if you can find the time to undertake practice exercises of this nature.

Sectioning your work appropriately

A key aspect of your work is setting it out in such a way that the reader is taken on a journey with you, the writer.

A useful analogy here is to consider the steps that you might take (before the onset of 'satnav' at least) if setting out to drive on an unfamiliar journey. You may well have consulted a road atlas and got the general idea of the direction you intended to travel, after which you are likely to have investigated the route in more detail, possibly noting specific road numbers and place names. It is probable that you would have given particular attention to places where the road number changed, or to complicated junctions. While travelling, you would find the presence of clear signposts helpful, giving you advance notice of junctions, clear directions and, possibly after complicated junctions, confirmation that you were still on the appropriate route.

It is very similar with academic writing. The reader needs to have a clear indication at the outset of the general route they are intending to follow, and then regular signposts in the 'journey' through your work of where they are, what is coming up, what to expect, and what stage of the journey they are at. You as the writer have a responsibility to place these signposts appropriately throughout your work, rather than expecting your readers to find their own way. Just as in the analogy of the road journey, you will have to give particular attention to places where the argument becomes complicated, or where perhaps you as the author (and therefore your readers) intend to by-pass an issue, perhaps to return to it at a later point in your argument. Your readers should always know, intellectually, where they are in your argument, what has been covered, and the direction in which they are travelling. These 'signposts' can take several forms in academic writing; for example:

- 'The discussion so far has revolved around the issues of . . .'

- 'The next chapter will further discuss the findings.'

- 'There are two key research questions in this investigation. The first key question is . . .'

- 'The second key research question is . . .'

- 'I turn now to consider . . .'

- 'In summary . . .'

The trick is to create a cohesive narrative without using clichés or unnecessary 'filler' phrases (see Chapter 8 for further tips and hints).

Creating cohesive chapters

The most obvious way of sectioning your work is through dividing it into chapters. There will usually be guidance on how to do this in the assignment booklet that you are given by your tutor. You should make sure to follow the guidance; the conventions we set out below simply give you one example of how this sectioning can be done within a dissertation/practitioner research assignment text:

Chapter 1: an introduction, in which you set out the general context of your work and what you hope to achieve. By setting out these details, you are giving the reader an indication of why your work is important, how it relates to previous work, and the scope and limitations of what you intend to argue. You may also touch on your own motivation for the work, but this should relate to other academic work and avoid becoming too 'personal'.

Chapter 2: a literature review, in which you place your research in the context of appropriate academic writing, and show how your work will contribute to a particular aspect of that context.

Chapter 3: an explanation of your methodology, in which you set out the specifics of your work, its rationale and the methodology.

Chapter 4: where you report on your research findings.

Chapter 5: a discussion in which you undertake a critical analysis, in which you analyse your findings as outlined in previous chapters, and relate them back to your literature review. It is possible to present Chapters 3 and 4 as one unitary chapter entitled 'findings and analysis'; it is not unusual for this to be the convention in your institution for studies that have used principally qualitative methods.

Chapter 6 (or 5 if you have written a findings and analysis chapter): where you draw conclusions and make recommendations. Your conclusions should be appropriate. For example, you should check that they are relevant to the issues that you have identified in your title and previous chapters. You need to ensure that your conclusions and recommendations are consistent with the evidence and arise from that evidence. Try to avoid making your conclusions too pompous or too trivial. For example, a study into a particular situation in one setting is not likely to be making a major contribution to the understanding of that situation nationally or internationally; on the other hand, an in-depth study into practitioners' use of information technology should conclude with something more substantive than the recommendation that teachers should discuss the use of information technology more at staff meetings. So, state your awareness of the status of your conclusions and recommendations, and identify perhaps where further work might need to be done (see Chapter 8 for further discussion of conclusion sections).

Activity

Pick one of our example students and bullet-point what content we might expect to find in each chapter, either as the chapters are outlined above, or in the format in which your dissertation module requires your write-up to be structured.

Reflection point

Which chapter do you think they might find the most difficult to write? If you have time, consider this question with respect to more than one of our example students, reflecting upon whether they might find different aspects more easy or difficult. Dissertations tend to be quite individual in this way, and it is impossible to predict how this will pan out for anyone at the beginning of the module, as there are so many variables that can make a difference.

Activity

Consider how these aspects 'made a difference' for our example students:

Ellie: attitudes from the management of the setting

Nick: his previous experiences of research and initial attitudes stemming from these

Florentyna: cultural and linguistic differences between herself and her colleagues

Sunil: his tendency to leave things until the last moment, and to seek an 'easy way out' of difficulties that subsequently arise.

Stylistic choices

Sub-headings

Within each chapter, sub-headings can be useful, although care should be taken to find an appropriate balance between, on the one hand, providing insufficient sub-headings and, on the other, providing too many. If there are too few or too many, the argument can become very difficult to follow.

Paragraphing

Careful paragraphing is also important. Here, again, you need to strike a balance between paragraphs which are too short (consisting of only two or three sentences, for example) and those which are too long (running over several pages). A paragraph should consist of a group of sentences which develop a particular theme or idea, and move your argument forwards. If you find this very difficult, ask your tutor or your librarian if your institution has a tutor who works with higher education students on their academic writing skills, and, if it has, make an appointment with that tutor to discuss this point.

Clarity of expression

One of the most challenging aspects of academic writing is expressing yourself clearly.

One of the keys to clarity of expression is being clear about what it is you want to express. This may seem like a statement of the blindingly obvious, indeed a truism, but a common fault in much poor academic writing is that it tends to obscure rather than reveal the main arguments. This means that, although you may not understand what you are trying to say when you start your work in your note-taking and your writing, you must be clear about it by the time you finish. Do not try to hide gaps in your understanding by writing convoluted sentences; if you do not understand what you are writing, there is very little chance that the reader of your work will be able to do so. In fact, it is very easy for an experienced reader or tutor to identify where a writer is writing without a full understanding of the issues or concepts. It may be relevant here to cite the expression: 'Mean what you say, and say what you mean.' The same point applies to academic writing that applies to charts and graphs - see Chapter 7 - if you are including a sentence that you don't really understand but think might impress the reader, the most likely result is the exact opposite. This also applies to using quotes when you are not quite sure what they mean, but look like they might just fit!

English may be an *evolving* language but it is not a *dissolving* one, so it is crucial that you write clearly, using Standard English, and using correct spelling and punctuation. It goes without saying that use of text speak or slang expressions will have the effect of severely limiting your grade, particularly in education studies/Early Years where the award of your degree will form at least part of the set of qualifications that are accepted as evidence of a person's competence to support children in the development of their literacy skills. Where students use their literacy skills most frequently for short electronic communications (e.g. text, Twitter) they can fall into the trap of using abbreviations without even thinking. If this describes you, do make sure to check your final draft very carefully.

When you are reading books and journals or, indeed, listening to music, what you are reading or listening to will probably appear to 'flow' naturally. What is not apparent are the many drafts of the work that have been crafted during the creative process. It is important to remember that drafting, editing and restructuring of your work are normal aspects of the writing process, and essential to make your line of arguments clear. Your work is likely to take a lot of drafting, so do expect to write and proof-read *all* of your chapters several times. Some students come into dissertation modules thinking that rewriting only occurs in connection with the literature review – this is not the case!

It is unlikely that the thoughts you have will come to you in exactly the most appropriate order. Therefore, a crucial aspect of writing is the willingness to accept the importance of proof-reading, and the importance of finding and correcting mistakes, as well as the willingness to delete sections of work that may become redundant as you work towards your final version. Just because you wrote something a few weeks or months ago does not mean that it automatically needs to find its way into your final version. Even if what you wrote previously was very good, it is possible that your subsequent writing means that earlier work should be revised.

Another saying that may feel daunting to you is the one which states: 'Genius is 99 per cent perspiration, and 1 per cent inspiration.' You may feel very far from being a genius and feel very unsure about getting started with your writing. But don't wait for inspiration before you start. If you do, you may be waiting for a long time. Better to start by putting in the 99 per cent perspiration. One reason for writing even when you feel that you have little worth writing about is that the very act of writing can help you to organise your thoughts and give you new ideas. A second reason is that, once you have something in writing, you can start editing it, adding to it, and so on.

Ellie

. . . reads the quotation below as she puts the finishing touches to her dissertation. She smiles and attaches it to an email that she sends to her tutor, thanking her for all her help. She writes on the email, 'This is just what I was like when I first started . . . desperate to be perfect, so afraid to make a start. I thought you might find this useful to use with next year's students.'

For many, one of the most daunting parts of academic writing is making a start. When faced with a blank piece of paper or, more likely these days, an empty 'virtual' piece of paper on a computer screen, it often seems that any thought is either too trivial to write, or too complicated and complex to be written. As a consequence, you may hesitate to write anything; the blank screen, or the blank page, can take on an almost intimidating air.

This type of fright was described vividly by Sir Winston Churchill in his book Painting as a Pastime *(Churchill, 1932), who described how his fear of a 'blank canvas' (literally, a blank canvas in this example) was dispelled only after someone else, noticing how hesitant Churchill was to make any mark on the canvas, picked up a large brush and applied 'several large, fierce strokes and slashes of blue on the absolutely cowering canvas', after which 'the canvas grinned in helplessness' before him.*

Interestingly, this example has a very physical quality to it. One can almost imagine the physical strokes of the paint brush on the canvas, and the energy and vitality involved. The physical energy involved in writing may be less (or, at least, different) but the excitement can be similar. An important part, therefore, of writing is making a start. Remember that what you write initially may well be poorly expressed, not worth writing, and may eventually be deleted. But by writing it, you 'break the spell' of the blank page, just as Churchill did. In fact, it can be useful to write anything, perhaps describing how you are feeling intimidated, just to get some text on the page, knowing full well that your early efforts will be deleted and that you are writing them only to get started. No-one else has to read your very early drafts. Once you have made a start, you can then begin to develop your thoughts.

Whatever the specific area of your work, it is likely that you will need to use some specialist terms or phrases. The general 'rule of thumb' is to remember that you are writing for an 'informed reader'. Where you use acronyms or abbreviations, you will need to make sure that you either provide a glossary or define the abbreviation the first time it is used. Beware of assuming that so-called acronyms, even if in common use, have the meaning usually ascribed to them: as one example, SATs is a colloquial term for National Curriculum tests in England, rather than a formal acronym. Another situation to consider carefully is where the acronym seems to have taken on a life of its own as a word, OfSTED being one such example.

Education makes use of many different acronyms and abbreviations. To those experienced in the immediate context, acronyms and abbreviations such as DfE, SATs, KS1, GCSEs, and even Early Years may need no explanation. There is a shared 'language-game' (Wittgenstein 1953). However, to those new to the context, or to those from other contexts (for example, the educational systems of other countries), these acronyms and abbreviations will probably require some explanation.

Reflection point

One of the writers of this chapter was once asked to review an Australian article for an international education publication. She recalls that she was soon completely lost, buried in the acronyms used by the author, which were not always fully translated. At times she couldn't even work out whether the writer was referring to primary or secondary education. It certainly made her think about how casually she would talk to colleagues about 'OfSTED; SATs; the EYFS; GCSEs; BAs; FDs; EYPs; EYPS . . . . This experience certainly made her more careful when using acronyms in her own writing.

Clearly, each chapter has a specific role in your work. However, there should be a narrative flow between each of them, so that, on reading the closing paragraph of one chapter, the reader is led into the opening paragraph of the next. The opening paragraph of each chapter will then take up the narrative, set out the purpose of the chapter, and identify key aspects of the structure.

When editing and proof-reading your work, it is helpful to be able to take some 'distance' from your work. This means reading it as your own severest critic, and reading what is actually on the page, rather than what you think is on the page. Academic writing and proof-reading are hard work; you need to be prepared to apply intellectual rigour to them as well as a scrupulous attention to accuracy.

The advice of a 'critical friend' can be helpful – someone you trust to give an honest opinion about your work (strengths and weaknesses) and who can come to it with a more detached eye than you as the writer. If you are a good organiser, perhaps you can persuade a group of students from your dissertation cohort to do this for one another.

Another way of developing a more detached view is to put your work to one side for a few days, and then re-read it; in doing so, you may well be able to spot sections that can be improved. Reading your work out loud (or getting a friend or a computer system to do so) may also help. One of the most common mistakes when writing is to forget to include something often quite central to the reader's understanding of the research and/or its context; this can emerge as a result of the writers becoming over-used to the material with which they are working. Developing your own critical eye, and making use of a critical friend can help to spot such omissions.

Finally, *never* take your dissertation to be bound after a re-drafting session in which you have corrected many errors. If at all possible, leave it at least overnight, and read through once more before committing to the binding process.

Referencing

As you know, part of your grade for your dissertation depends on the use that you have made of the relevant academic literature. This is important for several reasons. For example, you need to be aware of work that has already been done in your area of interest, so that you do not set out to do something that has already been done. Your awareness of existing work will also help you to place your ideas in the wider context. Another reason for reading the academic literature is that you may be able to extend existing work (even in a small way) and offer new insights, as your work develops from your stance 'standing on the shoulders of giants'.

As such, an important part of academic writing is the acknowledgement that you give to these others whose work has influenced your thinking. The fact that you have read widely in the area of your study, and have taken on board the arguments of others as well as possible gaps in the literature or of issues requiring attention, is a strength of academic work, and part of the skill of academic writing is *demonstrating* that you have looked critically at the theories and ideas of others working in your field of study and used these to construct your own debates and discussions. The details of references are provided to enable the reader to check the evidence upon which your arguments are based or to follow up further lines of enquiry.

Accurate and detailed referencing in academic work is not an optional extra, to be considered only as an afterthought (if at all) by the writer. It is, rather, an integral aspect of successful academic writing. Experience has shown that those who give this aspect of the work their careful attention are often those who produce the most successful pieces of academic work.

It should be remembered that all statements, opinions, conclusions, and lines of argument taken from another writer's work should be acknowledged, whether the work is directly quoted, paraphrased or summarised. Failure to do so may lead to accusations of plagiarism. The exact way you do this will vary, but a common device is to use single or double quotation marks to show direct quotes. Note that, when quoting, you must quote exactly. Sometimes there will be errors (for example, of spelling) in what you quote, but you should not correct these; instead you should write [*sic*] after the error to show that it is not your mistake. If you wish to omit part of the original source, you can do this by the insertion of ... to show where a section has been left out. Additions (to give a quotation sense in its new context in your work) should be indicated with the use of any additional words in square brackets.

The work to which you have referred in the text (internet sources, books, journals, papers, or other material) will need to be listed in a reference list at the end of your work. Again, the precise conventions will vary slightly according to the institution in which you are studying for your degree. You should therefore consult your institution's guidelines, and follow them exactly.

As well as referencing quotations, you should also acknowledge the sources of ideas. In general, ideas which are 'common knowledge' do not need referencing but ideas or lines of argument that have been suggested by others do.

This means, of course, that it is essential to keep an accurate and detailed record of your sources as you work. Software packages can help you, but of crucial significance (whether you use a software package or not) is your making an accurate record of your sources (see the record sheet template in Chapter 3). Get into the habit of doing the following whenever you access a source.

For **books**, record:

● The author's or editor's name and initials (and the name of the author(s) of the chapter(s) concerned if it is an edited book). (It is often helpful to record full names so that you remember whether the author is male or female, then you will know whether to refer to 'he' or 'she' proposes . . .)

- The year the book was published

- The title of the book (and the title and page numbers of the chapter if it is an edited book)

- Whether it is an edition other than the first

- The place in which the book was published

- The name of the publisher.

For **journal articles**, record:

- The author's name or names

- The year in which the journal was published

- The title of the article

- The title of the journal

- The page number(s) of the article in the journal

- As much information as you can find out about the journal, including the volume and issue numbers.

For **electronic resources**, record as much of the following as are available:

- The author's name or names

- The date of the resource used

- The title of the resource

- The edition if it states that it has been rewritten and not just revised

- The place of publication

- The name of the publisher

- The date you accessed the resource

- The electronic address or email

- The type of electronic resource (email, discussion forum, web page, CD-ROM, etc.)

- The page numbers from which you copied any information.

In writing your reference list, every detail should be correct, including author names, year of publication, and so on. It is also important to note the editions of any work, as changes to editions can be significant (Newman 2008).

A key reason for accurate referencing is that the readers of your work may wish to follow up a specific line of enquiry and being able to locate sources quickly is essential.

Secondary referencing

There may be occasions when it is difficult to find the original source of a quotation or a reference and you need to use a secondary source, which is where one author refers to the work of another. Wherever possible you should try to access the original source but, if it proves impossible, you should clearly indicate that you have *not* read the original piece of work and reference it appropriately. Remember, however, that such references rely on the author's giving an accurate reflection of the contents of the original work and that often authors interpret (or misinterpret) what they are reading to support their own arguments. It is also not unusual for authors to give an incorrect page number for quotations they use, so be very wary of citing these. Note that secondary referencing should be used very rarely, and preferably not at all (see Chapter 2).

Common conventions

Two common conventions that you may need to use are:

et al.   is an abbreviation meaning 'and others'. This is used when referencing a source by more than two authors in the main text. All authors must be listed in the list of references.

[*sic*]   means 'so' or 'thus', and is used when there is a mistake in the original text. It indicates that you have accurately quoted the original text and not made the error yourself. When you use direct quotations, you must reproduce the author's words *exactly*, including all italicisation, spellings, punctuation, and errors.

Appendices

Appendices are frequently found at the end of research reports and dissertations. What are they? It might be helpful to consider first what they are not. They are not the place to dump a whole lot of information of only passing importance to your main argument, but which you could not work out how to include in a chapter. Nor are they an opportunity for you to try to get around a word count by, for example, placing an outline of a particular learning theory in an appendix rather than summarising it within the body of the work. In such cases, the work will be marked as though it did not contain such an outline.

An appendix is however useful for including some complete tables of results, or transcripts of interviews, where in the relevant chapter you have been able only to show extracts. A good rule of thumb is that an appendix is a place for a reader to go for further information, for example if they have found a quotation from an interview particularly interesting, and opt to read the whole thing. What it absolutely is not is a place to put information which is vital to the reader's understanding of your data, discussions and/or analyses. A grade will inevitably suffer if the marker has to dig into your appendices for key information, and this is another common grade-limiting error in dissertations/practitioner research assignments. Some students say at this point, 'But the word limit was too short', to which the answer is: 'You need to re-write and summarise more succinctly.' In every batch of dissertations/practitioner research assignments, there will be some students who have managed to include the key information within the word limit, and who have used their appendices correctly, and some who have not. The key to a good grade is making sure that your dissertation is in the former category!

Conclusion

The key theme throughout this chapter has been to emphasise the need for accuracy and clarity. As your knowledge and practice skills increase, what may need to become more 'complicated' is not the writing in which you express your ideas, but the thought that goes into your work. This is the view of philosophy taken by Ludwig Wittgenstein in his work *Zettel* (Wittgenstein 1967), where he suggested that the purpose of philosophy is to untie the knots in our thinking, and that the result of philosophising is not another theory but rather the realisation that the knots in our thinking have been untied (Wittgenstein 1967: §452). However, he remarked that, in philosophy, our thinking needs to be as complicated as the knots it is trying to untie. This analogy can be extended to the broader field of academic writing as a whole; as the level of academic work becomes higher, the 'knots in our thinking' may well become more complicated and require more effort to untie. But untying them is the task of the academic writer, so that the reader is presented with a clear line of argument, however complicated the thinking has had to be to develop that clarity.

We hope that this book has not only helped you towards a good grade for your dissertation/practitioner research assignment, but also to untie some of these 'knots' in your own thinking about your practice. We wish you well in your degree studies as a whole, and hope that your tutors will soon welcome you back to carry out research at the next academic level. Rest assured that, if you have gradually developed your research skills by working through this book, you should find that you already have a comprehensive set of strategies to guide you through postgraduate research activities, and possibly one day to underpin an original piece of research that moves education into new and exciting arenas.

References

Churchill, W.S. (1950) *Painting as a pastime*, London: Whittelsey House.

Newman, S. (2008) Guidelines on referencing in academic writing, Bradford; Bradford College: http://www.bradfordcollege.ac.uk/eresources/documents/ReferencingGuidelines-v1.13.pdf [accessed 27 February 2012].

Wittgenstein, L. (1953) *Philosophical Investigations*, Oxford: Blackwell.

Wittgenstein, L. (1967) *Zettel*, Oxford: Blackwell.

Index